TRUST WORTHY

Building Healthy Relationships

by

Tim Shortridge

Trust Worthy:
Building Healthy Relationships

Copyright © 2020 Tim Shortridge

For our daughter, Melanie, and our son, Richard...
We love you both past anything.

Also by
Tim Shortridge:

Don't Cook Fish in the Company Microwave

Understand Accounting Without Falling Asleep

Understand California Sales & Use Tax

No Place to Run

Sealing Fate

Out of Plumb

Jake

Contents

Preface

A Quick Note on Learning

Have you ever read to the bottom of a page and realized you had no idea what you just read? I have. Many times.

In 1973, when I first began studying the material that would become this book, I found it helpful to read for understanding rather than just read. What I mean by this is I would visualize in my mind what I was reading, and I would use this visualization to test how well I understood it. I discovered that when I lost understanding, if I stopped reading and looked back, I could find where I lost it. Sometimes, I would have to backtrack a couple of pages, but I could always find where my understanding started to drift. In that area, I would find a concept I did not understand. And inside the author's description of that concept, I would find at least one word, and often many words, that I did not understand.

When I looked up these words in a dictionary, the concepts would come together, and I was able to visualize once again what I was studying.

There were so many authors who used words I did not understand, I started keeping a dictionary beside me whenever I read. Today, looking up words with an e-book is so much easier. I hold my finger on the word and my e-reader gives me the definition. So efficient.

If you notice any part of this book becoming a little fuzzy in your mind, I suggest you go back to the last part that made sense. Can you find a concept that was not clear? Is there a word within my description of that concept you are not sure of? Try looking it up and see if it helps.

If you think about it, doesn't it make sense? If I wrote in a language you did not know, you would not expect to understand anything you read. So, if I use a word you do not understand, why wouldn't it have a similar effect?

Study to Teach

In his book, *The 7 Habits of Highly Effective People*, Stephen R. Covey described another way to improve your understanding of what you study. Rather than study to learn, you could try studying to teach.

By studying with the intention of teaching someone else, you change how you view the material, and that viewpoint shift improves your ability to understand.

I have found this technique to be effective also. If you would like to try it, I suggest the following:

- Think of someone you know who could benefit from a better understanding of relationships.
- Contact them before you proceed and set up a time to meet within the next few weeks.
- While you study this book, take notes on how *you* will teach this material to *them*.
- Keep your appointment and teach them this material.

If you do, you both could benefit.

Study Groups

Forming a study group is another way to improve your understanding of what you read. When you invite people to join you in your studies, rather than reading to learn, you read to discuss. This viewpoint shift focuses your ability to understand, and the regular meetings can encourage you to continue to read and practice what you are studying.

A study group provides the added benefit of discussing the concepts with others and hearing their thoughts on what it means and how it might be applied in someone's life. It also provides a forum for practicing the material with friends and improving your relationships with them.

To form a study group, I suggest the following:

- Invite your closest friends to a weekly meeting to discuss this book.
- Limit the number of participants to eight. Anymore and the meetings will either take too long, or some of your friends will not have time to share their thoughts on the material.
- Have everyone read the first two chapters before the first meeting.
- Meet and discuss the *Study Group Questions* at the end of chapter two.
- Allow time for open-ended discussions outside of the *Study Group Questions*.
- Each week after that, read, practice, and discuss the next chapter or two.

TRUST WORTHY

Building Healthy Relationships

PART ONE:

THE FOUNDATION

<u>*Chapter 1*</u>

Overview

Hello. Thank you for peeking inside this book to see what I have to say. My name is Tim Shortridge, and I am writing this book because I believe it will help you build healthier relationships with the people in your life, especially those people who are most important to you, like your family, friends, and co-workers. For this book to do that, however, I must first try to build a healthy relationship with you.

As a writer, my relationship with you as a reader is significantly different from all other relationships in my life. The biggest difference is that the communication between us is strictly one-way, that is, from me to you.

I believe healthy relationships require mutual trust, and mutual trust requires communication which includes both talking and listening. Unfortunately, while you are reading this book, I cannot listen to you regardless how loud you speak or how hard I try. If we were sitting across from each other while I explained this material to you, and I never allowed you to ask questions or tell me your thoughts, I doubt if you would think very highly of me or this material.

After all, who likes to be lectured to?

To compensate for this one-sided communication, I will write in an informal style which I hope will be easy to understand. I will avoid jargon. I will use lots of examples, most from my own life. And I will include my contact information at the end, as I welcome your questions and thoughts.

My mother used to tell me one of the best ways to learn is by making mistakes. I may have taken her advice too literally for I have made many, many mistakes in my life (some I will use as examples of what not to do). However, my mother was right about learning from mistakes because my mistakes have taught me a lot, like how to marry my best friend and raise two amazing children. But the most valuable lesson I learned by making mistakes is the absolute, best way to learn is not by making mistakes, but by learning from the mistakes of others.

Therefore, I will explain what I have learned from my mistakes so you can learn from them without having to make them yourself.

For over forty-five years, I have attempted to improve the relationships in my life. Through research and observation, I looked for ideas I thought might help. And through trial-and-error, I tested those ideas to see if they worked. Of course, when I say *trial-and-error*, it was mostly *error* because most of the ideas I tried did not work. I am sure my family, friends, and co-workers would agree since I subjected them to my many failed attempts at using bad ideas to improve our relationships.

Many of the books I read over the years said, as humans, we seek out relationships with others because we benefit from them. That always sounded correct to me. I knew I had benefited financially from my business relationships. I also had benefited mentally from my school relationships. And I had benefited emotionally from my loving relationships. I also had ended many relationships over the years when I no longer felt like I benefited from them.

As I thought about this, it occurred to me a relationship could be called *healthy* if each party received benefits from the relationship that were greater than what that relationship cost them to maintain. For example, if you and I both feel like the benefits we receive from each other are worth more to us than the time and energy we spend on our relationship, then our relationship would be healthy.

I knew some of my longer-term relationships were healthy, but I had to admit others were not, and I wondered why some were better than others. Many of the books I had read said relationships required trust, and that made sense to me. If there was no trust, how could there be any relationship? But maybe trust was not enough.

Looking back on my life, I knew my healthiest relationship had always been with my wife, and we certainly trusted each other. Then it struck me, perhaps the key was we trusted *each other*. There was more than trust in our relationship, there was *mutual* trust. I wondered, could mutual trust be a requirement for a healthy relationship to exist?

If this were true, I saw two challenges with it.

The first challenge was I could not control people. I could not *make* them trust me. So, what could I do to *encourage* someone to trust me? The only thing I could think of, which I could control, would be making myself more worthy of their trust thereby encouraging them to trust me. So, how could I do that?

The second challenge I saw with mutual trust was how would I know if a person was worthy of my trust?

Eventually, I realized if I could resolve the second challenge, I would resolve the first because, if I could clarify the reasons why I should not trust someone, then I would also clarify what I would need to avoid doing to be worthy of other people's trust.

So, I asked myself, why would I not trust someone?

I managed to narrow my list down to five reasons. I would not trust someone who was dishonest, lacked integrity, showed no compassion, showed no empathy, or was not competent. And it would not matter what they might say as an explanation, I would not trust them (at least for now) because of what they did. It seemed to me anything someone might do that would lead me to not trust them could be included in one of these five general groups of actions.

For example, I did not trust a rude person, but rudeness could be viewed as not being competent at social interaction. Also, I did not trust an unreliable person, but not being reliable was a consequence of not keeping promises which would be a lack of integrity.

It made sense to me if I did anything within these five general groups of actions, people would not trust me either. Therefore, if I did the opposite of these five groups of actions, I would be more worthy of the trust of other people and thereby encourage them to trust me more.

My five trustworthy action groups became:

- Honesty – telling the truth
- Integrity – doing what I say I am going to do
- Compassion – showing I care by doing
- Empathy – listening to understand
- Competence – doing things correctly

So, to build mutual trust, all I had to do was to become more worthy of other people's trust by doing these five trustworthy groups of actions and then finding people worthy of my trust with whom I could build healthy relationships.

That sounded simple enough. As it turned out, it was not simple at all.

I quickly discovered there were three other abilities I needed to exercise before I could improve my five trustworthy action groups.

These three abilities were:

- Self-control
- Long-term perspective
- Self-awareness

Through trial-and-error (again, mostly error), I found when I did not exercise my self-control, I sometimes reacted to people without thinking and that destroyed the trust I had developed with them. When I did not think about a relationship with a long-term perspective, I did not make good decisions or expend the energy needed to exercise my self-control. And when I did not use my self-awareness, I did not notice when I was reacting until it was too late.

As I organized my thoughts, I realized these three abilities were a foundation that supports mutual trust, upon which healthy relationships could be built.

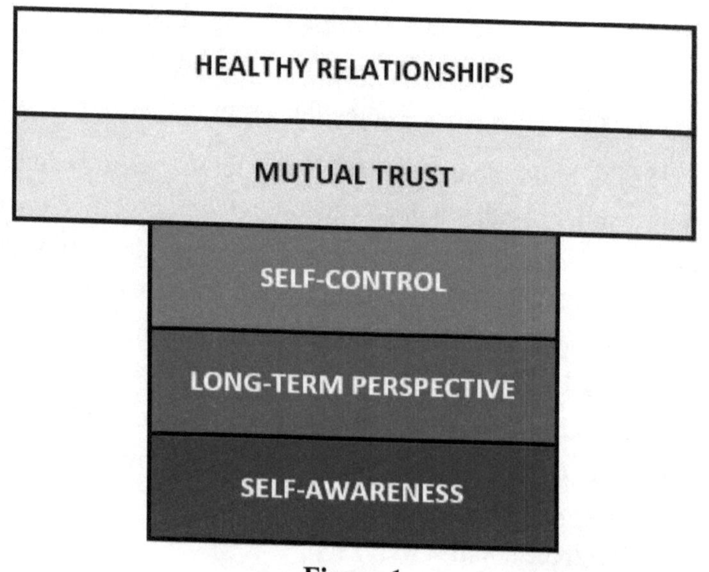

Figure 1

Figure 1 shows how they stack, one on top of the other, to form the layers of that foundation.

To build healthy relationships, I had to develop mutual trust. To develop mutual trust, I had to build a foundation that included exercising my self-control. To exercise my self-control, I had to develop a long-term perspective. And to develop a long-term perspective, I had to be self-aware.

In figure 1, I drew all three layers of this foundation with the same, narrow width because they all occur internally. In other words, being self-aware, thinking about things long-term, and controlling my actions all happen inside me without anyone else being involved. As I exercise these abilities, they provide the support I need to interact with people and develop mutual trust and healthy relationships.

I drew the mutual trust and healthy relationships boxes wider to represent how they extend out from me to other people.

For any structure to be solid, each layer must be strong enough to support the weight of all the layers above it. And to work, the layers must be built from the bottom up.

For example, I cannot build the roof of a house without first building walls that can support the roof, and I cannot build the walls without first building a foundation that can support both the walls and the roof.

Self-awareness, a long-term perspective, and self-control have been the foundation upon which I have built mutual trust. And it has been this mutual trust which has enabled me to build every healthy relationship in my life.

In each of the remaining chapters of Part One, I will focus on one layer of this foundation. I will start with the bottom layer, Self-Awareness, and work my way up.

In Part Two, I will discuss Mutual Trust and the five trust-worthy action groups required to create and maintain it.

In Part Three, I will discuss Healthy Relationships and what they look like.

As you study these different layers, please remember they are not all-or-nothing. Everyone can do each one of them at least somewhat, and no one is perfect at doing any of them, including me. I have found, though, as I have gotten better at doing each one, I have been able to improve the relationships in my life right away, especially those relationships that have mattered to me the most.

My Journey of Discovery

I was first introduced to some of these ideas in 1973 when I read Dr. Nathaniel Branden's book, *The Psychology of Self-Esteem*. Branden said that, as a human, I have the ability to be self-aware. He defined *self-aware* as the ability to not only live my life, but to be able to know I am living my life and to be able to observe myself living my life. No other living thing has this ability.

Branden went on to explain how being self-aware is not automatic like breathing or digestion. I have to choose to be self-aware. In addition, he said self-awareness is essential for taking control of my life.

When I read that, it reminded me of times growing up when I had felt out of control, like when I got angry and yelled at my brother or sisters. Most of those times, I was not self-aware. I was not even aware I was angry until I blew up. And once, when I was seventeen, I had broken up with my girlfriend without knowing why. It was not until later I realized I had been afraid our relationship was getting too serious.

Had I just not chosen to be self-aware?

Branden went on to explain how logic and reason are not automatic, either. Logic and reason require effort.

That got me thinking. Had I not been exerting the effort I needed to use my logic and reason? Possibly. After all, I was not raised to use logic or reason. I was raised to be a good Catholic and to do as I was told. If I did not do as I was told, I would burn in hell for all eternity.

While attending Catholic grammar school, most of the teachings made sense to me, like the ten commandments and the golden rule. Regardless if they made sense to me or not, I was instructed to believe everything they taught because if I did not believe…

Well, the consequences would be eternal.

I got quite good at accepting whatever I was taught, and it helped that there was nothing going on in my life to conflict with it.

That ended when I was sixteen and lost my virginity. For the first time in my life, I had sinned and was not sorry. There was no way I could go to confession, apologize, and promise to never do it again. I had every intention of doing it again whenever my girlfriend was interested.

I began to question my faith. Why would the church condemn an action that did not hurt anyone? It did not make sense to me. Then I wondered, why did I have to believe something just because a priest told me it was true? Would I really burn in hell for eternity? What if he were wrong?

My parents did not like me questioning Catholicism. So, I questioned them. Why should I do what they said unless it made sense to me? My dad, a career army pilot, did not like me questioning him. We argued a lot. And my mom was devastated by my dwindling faith and eventual eternal damnation.

By the time I graduated from high school a year later, I no longer considered myself a Catholic. Too much of the church's teachings made no sense to me, and I was no longer willing to believe. I had to be convinced.

During my first semester at the University of Maryland, I developed a passion for learning. In a philosophy class, we studied Rene Descartes' *Meditations on First Philosophy*, and I was struck by the brilliance of Descartes' thinking.

Descartes said the only thing we know for certain is we exist. That is because everything else we think we know comes from our senses. We only know the sky is blue because we see it. We only know fire is hot because we feel it. What if our senses were wrong? Since all our knowledge is based on our senses, if our senses were wrong, then all our knowledge would be wrong also. Except for the one thing that does not rely on our senses. We know we exist because we can think. If we did not exist, we could not think.

Between semesters, I read *Walden Two* by B. F. Skinner. I had never read a book before that was not required reading. I found it liberating to realize I could study anything. From then on, I read books constantly. Fiction, non-fiction, biographies, fantasies, it did not matter. I would read whatever I could find that looked interesting.

During the summer after my freshman year in college, I received my draft notice. Not wanting to carry a rifle around in the jungles of Vietnam, I enlisted in the Air Force.

While attending tech school for electronics and computer systems repair at Keesler Air Force Base outside of Biloxi, Mississippi, I spent my down time in the branch library just a couple of blocks from the barracks. I would look through the books and read whatever caught my eye.

One afternoon, I saw *The Fountainhead* by Ayn Rand. The title looked interesting, so I checked it out. The integrity of the main character amazed me. I wrote to my girlfriend (not the same girlfriend I had when I was sixteen) and suggested she read it. She wrote back she already had, and since I liked it, I should read Ayn Rand's *Atlas Shrugged*.

Since the branch library did not have a copy of *Atlas Shrugged*, I did not read it until after I graduated from tech school and was transferred to March Air Force Base, just outside Riverside, California. My girlfriend had sent me a Dear John letter by then, but I read the book anyway and it turned out to be another fascinating story filled with characters of uncompromising integrity. At the end of the book, Ayn Rand included a note praising Nathaniel Branden. That note led me to his book, *The Psychology of Self-Esteem*.

I am forever grateful to my ex-girlfriend for suggesting I read *Atlas Shrugged*. Kathy, if you ever read this, thank you.

Branden's book made me feel like I was beginning to understand myself and my relationships with others for the first time in my life. I wanted more.

The back flap of the book's dustcover said Dr. Branden had a private practice in Los Angeles. On my next day off, I drove to his office. I was not sure what I was hoping to gain by going there, but it felt like something I needed to do.

I took a seat in his waiting area without saying a word to anyone. When he entered and started talking to his receptionist, I just sat there, a frightened twenty-year-old too awestruck to speak. I could hardly breathe. I remember he was wearing red plaid pants, which I thought were odd, but it did not matter. I was sitting there in the presence of greatness.

After he went back into his office, I took a pamphlet from the coffee table and left. The pamphlet was from a mail-order bookstore that carried books which Dr. Branden recommended. His other book, *The Disowned Self,* was listed along with all of Ayn Rand's published works as well as other books on psychology, Objectivism, Libertarianism, economic theory, philosophy, and religion.

I spent my next paycheck ordering most of the books listed in the pamphlet. For months, I invested my spare time studying alone in the barracks. It was during this time I discovered the benefit of looking up words I did not understand as I described in the Preface.

While I studied in my room in the barracks, it seemed as if the world was going insane. Although the Vietnam War was winding down, the Middle East was heating up. Nixon was sworn in for his second term, seven Watergate conspirators were indicted, the vice president resigned, and OPEC imposed an oil embargo which sparked an energy crisis.

My job as an electronics and computer systems repairman was to maintain display equipment at the 15th Air Force Strategic Air Command. I had a top-secret security clearance and was exposed to lots of scary information, including the location of a Soviet submarine off the coast of Los Angeles. It carried a nuclear missile that could reach our location in about ten minutes.

That was why we always had a fully loaded B-52 bomber sitting at the end of our runway with a crew ready to take off in less than ten minutes.

I started to wonder if there was any way to make the world a better place. The peace and love movement of the 60's did not appear to have had much of an effect.

Then I thought perhaps it was not the world that was insane, just the people in it. And if that were true, maybe Nathaniel Brandon had the right idea. Maybe Psychology could fix the insanity of the world, one person at a time. So, I enrolled in Riverside City College to start working toward becoming a psychologist like Dr. Branden.

Although, I vowed I would never wear red plaid pants.

Unfortunately, the psychology they taught at the college did not jive with what I had been studying on my own, and my teachers quickly tired of my endless desire to debate.

Just before I dropped out of school, one of the drug users in the barracks (there were many in 1974) stopped smoking pot. He said the Church of Scientology helped him quit. Since it was a church, I was leery, but he said they did not ask him to believe anything. So, I went down to the mission to check it out for myself.

I found the introductory lecture interesting. The presenter discussed how better communication could increase understanding and improve relationships. After the lecture, I stayed behind and talked to him. He repeated I did not have to believe anything. What was true for me was what was true. So, I signed up for a course on communication.

Two weeks later, I met my future wife.

I saw Corky talking with one of the communication course supervisors during a break. I walked over and stood next to her. I felt awkward and stupid but was hoping she would introduce herself and include me in their conversation. After all, it was a course on communication. Corky turned and looked at me. I just stood there not knowing what else to do. Then she frowned and asked me what I was doing.

I took offense and made a crude remark.

You could say it was loathing at first speak. She thought I was an ass, and I thought she was a bitch. Oh well, I obviously still had a lot to learn about communication.

I started studying the books L. Ron Hubbard had written on Dianetics and Scientology. They contained many concepts with which I was already familiar. For example, Hubbard's *study tech* recommended looking up words not understood. I had been doing that for over a year. There were other familiar concepts which he described, but in ways that were different from what I had studied. Hubbard's idea of a *reactive mind* was similar to Freud's *id* in that Hubbard described the reactive mind as basic urges and emotions beyond our control, but Hubbard added the idea that these feelings come from past traumatic events during which we made decisions that still affect us.

Hubbard claimed to have the technology to rid people of their reactive minds, thereby helping each one of us become a better person. The idea of making people less reactive aligned well with my idea of making the world a better place by helping people one person at a time.

Unfortunately, this technology could only be studied on the advanced courses (which I could not afford). According to Hubbard, the technology was too dangerous to be available outside of the advanced courses because it could cause irreparable harm to an untrained reader.

That sounded a bit weird to me, but still, this group of highly motivated people, all of them around my age, were trying to help people. I started to think maybe I could help people without becoming a psychologist like Dr. Branden. Besides, if Scientology had a technology that was not available in any college, maybe I should study it first.

The Riverside mission was small, just two residential houses half a block apart, and Corky and I kept bumping into each other. Over time, our dislike began to wane. She was interested in what I thought about Hubbard's books (she was reading them, too), and I was interested in what her life was like working at the mission. We slowly became friends.

After a couple of lower-level courses, I jumped in and started working at the mission part-time in the evenings.

Corky and I eventually became best friends, and I moved out of the barracks and into a house she shared with half a dozen other Scientologists. The more time we spent together, the stronger our friendship.

By January of 1975, we were a couple.

A few months later, I received an honorable discharge from the Air Force and started working at the mission full-time. Working full-time meant working twelve to fifteen-hour days, six or seven days per week for little or no money. We were passionate and dedicated.

Corky and I were married in the Riverside Mission of the Church of Scientology in November of 1975. I was twenty-two, and she was twenty-one. To say we struggled to live would be an understatement. During the rare free time we had, we did any odd jobs we could find to pay for food and rent.

And the only thing we studied was Scientology.

* * *

By early 1980, Corky was pregnant with our first child and I needed to rethink my life. She had left staff, and I doubted if I could support us if I continued working at the mission. We were pretty much on our own because we had managed to alienate both our families over the years by trying to convince them of the awesomeness of Scientology.

As I reflected on the work I had been doing over the past five years, I realized I could not think of one person whose life was better because of Scientology. Even the drug user who had introduced me to the church had left years earlier and returned to using drugs.

I never took the advanced courses because I never made enough money to pay for them. But I knew quite a few members of the church who had taken the advanced courses, and they still seemed to act like they had reactive minds. It appeared to me that Hubbard's secret, so-called *technology* to rid people of their reactive minds did not work. And since that had become what was now true for me, then according to Scientology, it must have been true.

So, I quit and headed out into the job market with unknown skills and five years' experience working in a cult. Yeah, my resume looked great. After a few months, I managed to get my real estate license and became a mortgage broker, making just enough money for us to get by.

Our daughter, Melanie, was born in September of 1980, and our son, Richard, was born in April of 1982.

Using the GI Bill, I returned to college at night and eventually earned a bachelor's degree in Accounting, a far cry from the social sciences that had fascinated me before. But I enjoyed accounting, it made sense, and it was a career that would allow me to earn a living while helping people, even if I was not helping people in a *save the world* kind of way.

I also returned to studying on my own. Most of the books were business related or self-help. After all, I needed to make more money so I could better support my family.

For the next few decades, I searched for ideas that might help me advance my career. When I realized a business was nothing more than people working together to accomplish something, and it was the quality of the relationships the people had with each other that determined the success or failure of a business, I knew I needed to expand my study of relationships. I also realized some of the biggest blunders I had made in my career were not effectively managing my relationships at work.

I later recognized not only did the quality of relationships determine the success of a business, but they also seemed to determine the success of my life. My life always improved whenever the quality of my relationships with Corky, our children, or my co-workers improved. So, I decided I had to compile everything I had ever learned over the years and clarify what it was I needed to do to continue to improve the relationships in my life.

And that is how I arrived here, writing this book.

I do hope this information helps you as much as it has helped me.

Chapter 2

Self-Awareness

As I learned in 1973 from Nathaniel Branden's book, *The Psychology of Self-Esteem*, self-awareness is an ability I have that enables me to be aware of what is happening with me. In other words, not only do I live my life, I know I am living my life, I can observe myself living my life, and I can observe how I feel about living my life.

Branden pointed out that animals are not self-aware. They only act on instinct without being aware of what they are doing or how they feel about what they are doing.

I decided self-awareness had to be the first layer in the foundation that supports mutual trust because I had found whenever I did not exercise my self-awareness while interacting with people, I often reacted in ways that damaged the trust I had developed with them.

For example, when I first met my wife in 1974 and she asked me what I was doing, I suddenly felt intimidated and defensive for no apparent reason. Without being aware I was feeling these emotions, I reacted to them and made a crude remark. Corky immediately did not trust me.

In his book, Branden explained I have the ability to be self-aware, but it is not automatic. I must choose to be self-aware and then exert enough energy to pay attention.

However, I do not need to be self-aware all the time.

For example, when I ate breakfast this morning, I was reading a magazine and was not trying to be aware of myself eating or how I felt about it. Since I was not interacting with anyone, I did not need to exert the energy needed to be self-aware. I still paid attention to what I was doing (so I would not dribble on my shirt), but I did not need to be self-aware.

I had noticed my ability to be self-aware includes both noticing myself doing things externally as well as noticing the thoughts and emotions I experience internally.

Here is an example of external self-awareness. Right now, your eyes are moving from left to right as you read these words. Because I just pointed that out, your external self-awareness of reading probably kicked in. You can observe your eyes moving from left to right as your mind combines the meaning of the words into ideas. Not only are you reading, you are now observing yourself reading.

To experience internal self-awareness, take a moment and shift your attention internally to any thoughts or emotions you may be having right now. Do you feel confused, or light-headed, or angry, or curious? Are you enjoying this experience? This is internal self-awareness.

Turning on my self-awareness felt a bit weird the first time I tried it. And yet, improving my use of this ability was the first step to improving my relationships.

As I practiced my self-awareness, I found internal self-awareness to be more important to building healthy relation-ships than external self-awareness because I needed to use my internal self-awareness to monitor any thoughts or feelings that might lead me to react in an untrustworthy way.

For example, as I ate breakfast this morning and was reading without any self-awareness, Corky entered the kitchen and asked me for my opinion about a problem she had at work yesterday. Because she spoke to me, I turned on my internal self-awareness and immediately noticed I felt annoyed she had interrupted my reading. Rather than reacting by peering over my glasses at her with an annoyed expression, I took a moment to notice the annoyance, analyzed it as illogical because my wife is far more important to me than any article I might be reading, and then chose a better response. I set the magazine down, looked up at her, smiled, and asked her to tell me about what had happened.

This morning's interaction was quite different than when we first met. I have learned a few things over the decades we have been together, and sometimes, I even get it right.

Over time, I found building a healthy relationship requires many constant, thoughtful, trustworthy actions. Whereas destroying a relationship can be done quickly with just a few thoughtless, untrustworthy reactions.

If I hope to avoid reacting to my thoughts and emotions, I first must use my internal self-awareness to recognize when I am feeling them.

As I mentioned, I do not have to be self-aware every minute of every day. There are occasions when I get caught up in the moment and lose all track of time. If I am working on a project or reading a book, my attention can become absorbed in what I am doing without any thought about the fact I am doing it or how I feel about it. That is fine. It is not likely to harm my relationships.

However, whenever I interact with someone, I must fully engage my internal self-awareness and constantly monitor how I feel, analyzing if my thoughts and emotions make sense with what is happening around me. If my thoughts or emotions do not make sense, then I need to pause long enough to avoid reacting to them, choose how I should respond, and then act on that choice.

I have to remind myself self-awareness is not automatic. I must choose to observe myself and then exert enough energy to pay attention. And like any other activity, the more I have done it, the better I have gotten at doing it.

You may be wondering about these thoughts and emotions that can cause me to react. Where do they come from? The two most common sources are my:

- DNA-soup
- Historic Baggage

DNA-Soup

It took over three billion years for our ancestors to evolve from single celled organisms into self-aware humans (or at least occasionally self-aware humans). Of course, the self-awareness part did not happen until quite recently. So, during most of the time our DNA was evolving, our ancestors had been unaware of their own existence.

During the most recent few million years, our ancestors had been animals, struggling to survive in hostile environments. Those best at surviving long enough to procreate, had passed on their DNA to their children. Each subsequent generation had then become more and more hard-wired to survive and have children because whoever had been best at doing those two things passed on the most DNA.

Through periodic DNA mutations, new abilities had been introduced to our ancestors. Whenever a new ability had given someone greater success at surviving and having children, they would pass on more of their DNA than those who had lacked that new ability.

Eventually, one of our ancestors had been born with a mutation that allowed him (or more probably her) to be self-aware. And that enhanced ability to think had proven to be helpful in both surviving and having children. That was the reason why all our most recent ancestors had the ability to be self-aware.

I inherited this entire evolutionary soup of DNA from my parents. This DNA-soup includes mostly survive-and-have-children oriented DNA with just a little you-can-be-aware-of-yourself DNA sprinkled in at the end.

These urges to survive (eat! fight! run!) and have children (sex!) are strong. I feel them in my core.

Why does the advertising adage *sex sells* work so well? Because sex communicates to our most basic DNA-self. The urge to have children is powerful, and yet most people are unaware it is influencing their thoughts and emotions.

Whenever I have been under the influence of the sexual urges of my DNA-soup, staying self-aware enough to pause and think about the possible long-term consequences of giving in to those urges required tremendous effort. Anyone who has ever had to pause long enough to find a condom, knows exactly what I am talking about.

The physical and emotional feelings generated by my survive-and-have-children DNA are beyond my control, and yet I feel them every day. As my body interacts with the world around me, my DNA-soup instinctively tries to steer me into doing whatever I have to do *right now* to survive and have children. And if I am not self-aware enough to recognize it, then I run the risk of reacting to it in ways that can damage my relationships.

Historic Baggage

Unfortunately, my DNA-soup is not the only thing generating internal thoughts and emotions that try to steer me into reacting in ways that can damage my relationships. My personal history can also influence how I feel.

For example, if I was shunned by the popular kids in high school, as an adult, I may feel anger towards anyone at work who has a lot of friends, and I may only feel comfortable around other people who are less social like me. And if I had decided back in high school I was not worthy of anyone's friendship because I was being shunned, then that decision could have an even greater impact on how I feel now. I might not bother to try and make friends, and my lack of friends could then support my belief that I am unworthy of friendship. I may even act like a jerk to push people away before they can push me away, thinking I would rather do the rejecting than be the rejected.

My historic baggage is made up of all the painful events I have ever experienced along with any decisions I may have made during them. It generates thoughts and emotions in response to what is happening around me whenever what is happening around me is similar to what has happened in my past.

Although I feel these thoughts and emotions in the present, they are in response to my past experiences and may not make sense in response to what is currently happening. Just because I was shunned by the popular kids in high school does not mean I will be shunned currently by the employees at work who have a lot of friends.

A Dangerous Partnership

My historic baggage of past experiences and decisions sometimes joins forces with my DNA-soup. This can occur whenever something is happening around me which my DNA-soup interprets as threatening my life or ability to have children and is also similar to an earlier painful event in my life. When this happens, I can experience powerful physical and emotional feelings.

If I am unaware of these feelings, I can easily react to them rather than using my logic and reason to determine how best to respond.

For example, when Corky and I first met, she asked me, "What are you doing?" In that instant, my DNA-soup interpreted her question as a challenge and its *fight! run!* impulses flared. I felt a physical pulling back. Plus, my historic baggage, containing all the rejection I had ever experienced before in my life, joined forces with my DNA-soup and together they ignited a flash of powerful emotions.

I reacted to these feelings without thinking. Why? Because I was not aware of what was happening to me. I was not paying attention to how I was feeling. If I had been self-aware enough to realize I was feeling the effects of my DNA-soup (fight! run!) and historic baggage (prior rejection, feeling unworthy), I could have paused long enough to think about how I should respond. Instead, I just reacted.

During breakfast this morning, however, I used my self-awareness and avoided a reaction that could have damaged our current relationship.

Just because I feel something does not mean I have to react to it. But I probably will if I am not aware the feeling is coming from my DNA-soup or historic baggage.

I still struggle with being self-aware whenever I am tired, distracted, or especially passionate about something. That is when I can slip into old habits and react based on how I feel. You would think I would have conquered this by now, but it has never been easy. Whenever I am not at my best, I must remind myself to pay closer attention to how I am feeling and what is causing those feelings.

This was especially true after we lost our son in 2008. I had never realized how painful self-awareness could be. Observing myself grieving was a continuous reminder of the depth of my loss. And yet, had I not observed myself being in that depressed state and reminded myself to pause and think before reacting, I can only imagine how much damage my poor behavior could have caused. Do not get me wrong, I was no saint during that time, and I messed up a lot, but it could have been much worse.

The coroner told us many marriages end in divorce after the loss of a child. We did not allow that to happen to us, but it took a lot of self-awareness.

I was determined to gain control over how I responded to the people in my life. And I knew the first step in that process would be to stay self-aware enough to spot the physical and emotional feelings and thoughts generated by my DNA-soup and historic baggage whenever I was interacting with someone.

Summary

I made self-awareness the first layer of the foundation that supports mutual trust because without it, I do not recognize the thoughts and feelings that can lead me into reacting in ways that can damage my relationships.

I experience physical and emotional feelings and thoughts in response to what is happening in my life. These feelings and thoughts are out of my control and may not make sense to me based on what is happening now. They commonly come from my:

- DNA-soup – evolutionary urges to survive and have children
- Historic baggage – past painful experiences and the decisions I made during them

* * *

Before reading the next chapter, you might want to try this Self-Awareness Exercise:

Self-Awareness Exercise

1. Agree to exercise your internal self-awareness for the next 24 hours whenever you are with someone.
2. Use your self-awareness to observe yourself making this agreement with yourself. Are you committed to doing it? Do you feel any emotional or physical reaction to the idea of doing this exercise? Does it make sense to you that you feel this way?
3. Use a self-awareness reminder by selecting an object you can wear on your finger or wrist. A ring or watch band will work, but do not use the watch face or people might think you are checking the time. I use my wedding ring.
4. Look closely at your reminder object and observe yourself looking at it. Study its color, texture, size, and shape. Observe yourself studying it.
5. Now observe how you feel internally. Are you feeling any emotions? How do you feel about your

reminder object? How are you feeling about doing this exercise?

6. Tell yourself to observe yourself internally every time you see your reminder object. Observe yourself telling yourself this. How are you feeling about telling yourself this?

7. Look away, then back at your reminder object. Tell yourself again to observe yourself internally every time you see it and observe yourself telling yourself this again. Stop when you feel comfortable about this agreement with yourself.

8. Whenever you are with someone, periodically glance at your reminder object, observe how well you are maintaining your internal self-awareness. Are you feeling any inappropriate emotions? If so, are you able to avoid reacting to them? If you cannot avoid reacting, then excuse yourself and leave.

9. Notice if your self-awareness drifts away. Are you distracted or lost in thought? Do you feel anything that does not make sense to you?

10. At the end of 24 hours, reflect on your experience observing yourself with others. What did you learn?

11. Repeat steps 1-11.

Study Group Questions

1. How can we help each other exercise our internal self-awareness during these meetings?

2. What might happen to our lives if we regularly give in to our DNA-soup urges to survive (eat, fight, run) and have children (sex)?

3. Would anyone like to share a decision you made in your past that has caused you to feel emotions or thoughts about things that happened recently, but did not make sense with what was happening?

4. Did anyone notice feeling any illogical emotions while practicing self-awareness this past week? Do you think the reactions came from your DNA-soup or historic baggage?

5. Would anyone like to share your experience with the Self-Awareness Exercise?

Chapter 3

Long-Term Perspective

A long-term perspective is thinking about my relationships as if they will last a long time, and then making decisions based on that thinking. I made it the second layer in the foundation that supports mutual trust because it helps me make better relationship decisions.

While interacting with others, I try to use my internal self-awareness to spot any thoughts or emotions that might cause me to react in ways that can damage my relationships. And then, to avoid reacting to those thoughts and emotions, I try to pause long enough to use my logic and reason to decide how best to respond. Whenever I have used a long-term perspective when deciding how best to respond, I have tended to choose better responses.

For example, when Corky interrupted me at breakfast the other morning, I could have reacted to the annoyance I felt. But that annoyance was only a temporary feeling generated by my DNA-soup or historic baggage. Rather than react, I decided it would be better in the long-term if I treated her with love and respect, which was a much better response.

Since I define a healthy relationship as one where both parties receive greater benefit than the time and energy their relationship costs them, I know a healthy relationship will tend to last a long time simply because both parties will want it to continue. Therefore, it makes sense to me to think about a relationship as if it will last a long time.

As I interact with others, however, I frequently feel thoughts and emotions that steer me toward short-term thinking because my DNA-soup is all about Eat now! Fight now! Run now! Have sex now! And my historic baggage wants me to react now to things that happened years ago, regardless of the consequences those actions might have on my relationships. They are both short-term oriented.

Whenever I have considered giving in to the feelings generated by my DNA-soup or historic baggage, my thoughts tended to sound something like this:

> *Should I eat that donut? Sure. I could use the comfort, and I deserve it anyway.*

> *Should I have a cigarette? Why not? I could get hit by a bus and die tomorrow.*

> *Should I party tonight or go to sleep and be rested for work tomorrow? Party! Tomorrow will take care of itself.*

> *Should I read the parenting book my wife gave me or watch TV? Watch TV. I need time to relax.*

If I could not think of a good reason to justify my short-term pleasure seeking, society had plenty:

> *You only live once, make the best of life now! Life is short. Live for today!*

Who knows what tomorrow may bring?
Let's just do it!

To battle short-term urges, I had to develop a long-term perspective. Ironically, it takes a long time for the human brain to develop the ability to think long-term. That is why a child thinks an hour is *forever*. And to a teenager, a week is way too long to have to wait for anything. Adults, however, can start to think in terms of months and then years. And by the time we reach seventy, months seem to fly by, and a decade does not seem long at all.

I grew up in the 1960's with the threat of nuclear war hanging over my head. In my teens, I did not expect to see twenty. If the Soviet Union did not nuke us, I would probably be drafted and die in the jungles of Vietnam. And since my dad was an army pilot, we moved a lot. I attended four different high schools before I graduated. During my senior year, my perspective was definitely not long-term.

TIMOTHY DOUD SHORTRIDGE

Make the best of the present, because the past can never be relived and the future is nothing more than a dream.

That senior quote of mine says:
> *Make the best of the present, because the*
> *past can never be relived and the future is*
> *nothing more than a dream.*

It was a good thing I did not take my own advice for I am currently living in that future which my seventeen-year-old self said was nothing more than a dream.

If I had never said *no* to short-term pleasure seeking, my current life would most likely be quite different than it is now because I would be living with all the consequences of my poor decisions. I would probably be bankrupt, divorced, obese, and have no friends or family who want anything to do with me simply because I always sought short-term pleasure.

The biggest problem with a short-term perspective is that the worst thing that can happen to someone who lives their life that way is for them to live a long time. What kind of a life could I possibly create for myself if my worst-case scenario is living long enough to get old?

I did not start to develop a long-term perspective until three years after high school when I read *The Psychology of Self-Esteem*. Although I had avoided Vietnam, survived to be twenty, and the Soviet Union did not appear eager to launch a first strike, I was not happy with my relationships in the Air Force or my life in general. I wanted to do something with my life that might help make the world a better place. So, I began to imagine what my life might be like if I became a psychologist.

That was the first time I had ever looked at anything with a long-term perspective.

Even after I began to develop a long-term perspective, my plans continued to change as I discovered what worked for me and what did not.

For example, a year after I had decided to pursue becoming a psychologist, I decided I would try to make the world a better place by helping people get rid of their reactive minds by joining Scientology and dropping out of college.

After Corky got pregnant in 1980, however, my plans changed again, and not just career-wise but on a personal level as well. I was about to become a father. I not only needed to make more money to support my family but riding around on my motorcycle would no longer be an acceptable activity (I never owned a helmet). My unborn child's future would be better if I avoided dying.

Even after I thought I was on the right path to improving my life, I still struggled with short-term emotions. In my late twenties and early thirties, I was working two jobs and going to college four nights a week. If I was not working or in class, I was studying. I had little time for my wife and children. My greatest fear was I would die before we could enjoy any of the benefits we had envisioned. I frequently felt I should drop out of school again so I could enjoy my life a little.

But a long-term perspective helped me to battle those feelings for I knew my family would be better off long-term if I did not quit. As it turned out, all that work did pay off.

Human Abilities

In his book, *The 7 Habits of Highly Effective People*, Dr. Stephen R. Covey described four abilities that are uniquely human and could help me to better develop a long-term perspective.

These four uniquely human abilities are:

- Self-Awareness
- Imagination
- Conscience
- Independent Will

Self-Awareness

As I discussed in the last chapter, I put exercising my ability to be self-aware as the first layer in the foundation that supports mutual trust because without self-awareness, I do not notice thoughts and emotions that can lead me into reacting in ways that can damage my relationships.

As it turned out, self-awareness is also the first ability I needed to use to develop a long-term perspective for it enabled me to evaluate my relationships as they were currently and to observe how I felt about them. When I took a moment and thought about my relationships as they were, I knew they needed to improve. They did not seem healthy to me, and I did not feel good about them. This self-awareness of my need to change then led me into thinking about what I might be able to do to improve my relationships.

That thought process required me to use my imagination.

Imagination

Imagination is my ability to visualize something that is not present, even something that has never existed.

For example, I can imagine a pink elephant by visualizing it in my mind. I can then imagine it growing an extra trunk. Then another one. Using my imagination, I can visualize a pink elephant with three trunks.

By using their imaginations, people can visualize things that might be. They can also think about solutions to problems no one else has ever considered.

For example, there once lived an unknown technical clerk who worked in a Swiss patent office. Ever since he was quite young, this clerk had been using his imagination to do what he referred to as thought experiments. In 1905, he wrote a paper about one of his thought experiments where he examined the difference in perspectives between a man on a moving train and a man standing beside the track. How might they each view a bolt of lightning that struck two trees, one on either side of the man by the tracks? By using his imagination, this patent office clerk analyzed the relationship between space and time which he called the special theory of relativity. This thought experiment led him to the mathematical conclusion that matter and energy are related. He expressed this conclusion with the formula $E = mc^2$. His name was Albert Einstein, a very imaginative guy.

Prior to someone creating something, they must imagine it first. Every invention, from the first wheel to the internet, was imagined in someone's mind before it was built.

For example, the last time I cooked something, I imagined the completed meal in my mind before I pulled the ingredients out of the pantry. Even though I ended up with something quite different from what I had originally imagined (because I am a lousy cook), I still had used my imagination before I started to create the meal.

Imagination was the second ability I needed to use if I wished to develop a long-term perspective. Self-awareness had enabled me to evaluate my relationships as they were and observe how I felt about them. Imagination then enabled me to visualize how my relationships could be and how I might feel about them if they were different.

When I used my imagination to visualize how my life might be in thirty years if my relationships stayed as they were, I was not happy with what I thought that would look like. Then I visualized my life in thirty years if I improved my relationships. That looked much better.

The next step would be to use my conscience and decide if improving my relationships was the right thing to do.

Conscience

Conscience is that little voice inside my head that tells me what is right and what is wrong.

Animals have no concept of right or wrong. They react on instinct to compete for survival. Whether their actions are ethical or not does not factor into what they do. They do whatever they *can,* right now, to survive and reproduce.

As a human, though, I can think about what is right and what is wrong because I have a conscience. Without self-awareness and imagination, however, the concept of right and wrong would have no meaning. Using self-awareness and imagination, I can think about the long-term consequences of my actions and then decide if I *should* do something or if it would be better if I did something else.

Listening to my conscience was the third ability I needed to use if I wished to develop a long-term perspective. Self-awareness enabled me to evaluate my relationships as they were and observe how I felt about them. Imagination enabled me to visualize how my relationships could be and how I might feel about them if they were different. And then, my conscience helped me evaluate my possible actions and decide which ones I *should* take.

I noticed there was a big difference between something I thought I *wanted* to do and something I thought I *should* do. What I wanted to do tended to fall into the category of short-term thinking. While what I felt like I should do implied a more long-term perspective and commitment.

For example, when I had felt overwhelmed by work and night school, and I wanted to drop out and enjoy my life a little, it was my conscience that whispered to me that I should stay in school and get my degree.

It was also my conscience that told me I *should* work to improve my relationships; it was the *right* thing to do.

After I knew I should improve my relationships, I then needed to use my independent will and decide to do it.

Independent Will

Animals do not choose what they are going to do. They just react on instinct. As a human, however, I have the ability to choose what I am going to do. That does not mean I always listen to my conscience and choose wisely, but I do choose my actions. I can even choose to do nothing, but it is still a choice I make. This is my independent will.

If I were to use my self-awareness to observe my relationships as they are, use my imagination to visualize them being better in the future, listen to my conscience and realize improving them is something I should do, then I could use my independent will and decide to take the action I needed to improve them.

Of course, I found deciding to do something long-term, and then doing it long-term are two different things entirely. Independent will enables me to decide to do something, but it also enables me to change my mind and decide not to do it later. That is why my New Year's resolutions had been so quickly abandoned. Doing something I decide to do long-term requires me to exercise my self-control.

I will discuss self-control in depth in the next chapter. For now, I just want to point out the difference between deciding to do something and then doing it.

Part of the difficulty with long-term plans is the short-term nature of decision making. Every day, I make hundreds of decisions as I live my life. When should I get up? Should I take a shower? What should I wear? Should I have breakfast?

What should I eat? All day long, I decide one thing after another until I finally decide to go back to bed.

Each decision is made at that moment. I may have planned my day the night before, but I still must decide each moment of the day if I am going to follow my plan. All the while, I feel the thoughts and emotions of my DNA-soup and historic baggage trying to steer me into short-term reacting. Hundreds of times a day, as I confront each new decision, I must resist giving in to these physical and emotional feelings. Only if I make enough good decisions and act accordingly will I make any progress toward my goals.

To make any significant progress, I must use my self-awareness to monitor how I feel and use a long-term perspective to choose the actions I *should* take in each situation. And then, I must decide to exercise enough self-control to take those actions.

Corky and I spent years supporting each other through night school by using a shared long-term vision for our future. We made tens of thousands of daily decisions and had to constantly exercise our self-control to stay on track. It was not easy, but it was achievable. And it certainly paid off.

I made self-awareness, a long-term perspective, and self-control the three layers of the foundation that supports mutual trust because they are all essential to the development of mutual trust, but they also rely on each other.

I knew self-awareness and a long-term perspective were essential for me to exercise my self-control. That was why I put them as the first two layers of the foundation that supports mutual trust. Unfortunately, I quickly learned I needed to exercise at least some self-control if I wanted to use my self-awareness and develop a long-term perspective.

Luckily, I found developing my self-awareness and a long-term perspective did not require that much self-control, and the more I developed them, the greater my desire was to improve my self-control even further.

Summary

A long-term perspective is thinking about my relationships as if they will last a long time. I made it the second layer in the foundation that supports mutual trust because it helps me make better relationship decisions.

As a human, I possess four uniquely human abilities that enabled me to develop a long-term perspective:

- Self-Awareness
- Imagination
- Conscience
- Independent Will

I developed a long-term perspective by using my self-awareness to evaluate my relationships as they were, used my imagination to visualize how they could be better in the future, listened to my conscience to determine if I *should* make them better, and then used my independent will to decide I would make them better. Once I made that decision, I then used my self-control to act on that decision.

*   *   *

Before reading the next chapter, you might want to try this Long-Term Perspective Exercise:

Long-Term Perspective Exercise

1. Assume you will live to be 100. Nothing you do will kill you or put you in a coma, but you will experience all the other consequences of your actions. If you chain smoke, lung cancer will not kill you, but you will be fighting to breathe for the last couple of decades of your life. If you eat poorly and do not exercise, your body will deteriorate, you will have difficulty moving, and you will develop constant pain. If you drink too much, cirrhosis of your liver will result in fatigue, weakness, itching, and easy bruising. Regardless what you do, you will live to be self-aware until your 100th birthday.

2. Using your internal self-awareness, how do you feel about this idea of living to be 100? Why?

3. Think about your future. Between now and your 100th birthday, what kind of relationships do you want to have? What kind of a person do you want to be?

4. Make a list of a few things you would like to do differently between now and your 100th birthday.

5. Choose one thing on your list and do it differently for the next 24 hours.

6. Maintain your self-awareness each time you choose to do this one thing differently. Do you have any

physical or emotional feelings, especially any that do not seem to make sense to you?

7. At the end of 24 hours, reflect on your experience of doing one thing differently. What did you learn?
8. Make any changes to your list based on what you have learned.
9. Repeat steps 5-9.

Study Group Questions

1. Why is self-awareness important to developing a long-term perspective?
2. Can anyone imagine what your life might be like with healthier relationships?
3. Would anyone like to share a time you benefited from listening to your conscience? How about a time you suffered because you ignored it?
4. Would anyone like to share your struggle with sticking to a plan in the face of daily decisions?
5. Would anyone like to share your experience with the Long-Term Perspective Exercise?

Chapter 4

Self-Control

I define self-control as the practice of deciding how I want to act and then acting in the way I decide. It is the opposite of me thoughtlessly reacting to my DNA-soup and historic baggage.

If I wanted any chance at becoming worthy of people's trust, I had to improve my self-control. And to improve my self-control, I had to learn to identify those things I could not control and separate them from those things I could control. Once I did that, then I needed to focus my attention on those things I could control.

One thing I could not control were the feelings coming from my DNA-soup and historic baggage.

Those feelings occur when something is happening around me that is similar to something that happened in my past. An urge to fight-or-run can kick in, adrenaline will start pumping, and anger or fear will flood my senses. There does not appear to be any way I can stop these feelings from happening. And I have not found anyone who has figured out how to stop them. Sigmund Freud thought he had a solution, and L. Ron Hubbard claimed to have one too. But neither of their solutions seem workable to me.

Perhaps someday, someone will find a way to rid us all of the feelings generated by our DNA-soup and historic baggage. Until then, I think the best we can do is to learn how to stop reacting to them.

Luckily, experiencing the feelings generated by my DNA-soup and historic baggage does not harm my relationships. Sure, those feelings can be strong, they even seem overwhelming at times, but they are still just feelings. They take place inside of me, and if I do not react to them, they cannot harm my relationships.

For example, when Corky interrupted me reading a magazine at breakfast the other morning, I felt annoyed. But Corky was not affected by that feeling because I did not react to it. When I first met her in 1974, however, I did react to the feelings I experienced, and how I reacted back then definitely affected my relationship with her.

It has taken me decades of practice to get my self-control to where it is today. I am still far from perfect at using it, but I am way better than I was in 1974.

Even though I did not have control over the physical and emotional feelings generated by my DNA-soup and historic baggage, I knew if I could somehow avoid reacting to them, then I should be able to gain control over my responses.

Like most people, I am terrified of public speaking. Unlike most people, I made myself do it anyway. My DNA-soup and historic baggage pumped out fear trying to stop me from getting in front of people, but I decided I would choose my response and not let my DNA-soup and historic baggage control my life. For twenty years, I taught business workshops despite the fear I felt every time I did it.

Animals react on instinct to their environment. They do not think about how they should respond. Their entire lives are outside of their control. But I knew I was not like animals. I had the ability to control my responses, even if I rarely used that ability. I just needed to figure out how to do it.

It took me a long time to sort out what I could do to improve my self-control, but I eventually came up with five steps that work better for me than anything else I have tried. Whenever I feel any physical or emotional feelings that might be coming from my DNA-soup or historic baggage, I try to follow these five steps *in order*:

1. Self-awareness – use it to recognize when my DNA-soup and historic baggage are generating physical or emotional feelings to what is happening around me.
2. Pause – before I react to anything I may be feeling.
3. Evaluate – use my self-awareness during a pause to measure the intensity of my feelings and then the accuracy of my understanding of what is happening around me.
4. Choose – the best response using a long-term perspective.
5. Respond – do what I have chosen to do.

Self-Awareness

The first step in gaining control over how I responded, rather than reacting to the physical and emotional feelings that might have been coming from my DNA-soup and historic baggage, was to observe I was feeling them.

For example, if I am passing a donut shop right after lunch, and I suddenly feel the desire to eat an apple fritter, I must exercise my self-awareness enough to realize the desire to eat when I am not hungry does not make sense. If I do not exercise my self-awareness enough to realize this, then I have no chance to control my response. I might stop and buy two apple fritters, or maybe a dozen, and there goes my New Year's resolution to lose weight.

Every day, my DNA-soup and historic baggage tries to influence my actions. These physical and emotional feelings are beyond my control. I cannot stop them. By being aware of them, though, I can prevent them from determining how I will respond.

I was happy when I learned I do not have to react immediately to how I feel. That immediate reaction is usually wrong anyway, especially when my feelings are coming from my DNA-soup and historic baggage. Instead, I can use my self-awareness and decide if my physical and emotional feelings make sense with what is happening.

For example, if I feel a dreadful fear when a rattle snake slithers out from under a bush and moves toward me, I know immediately that desire to run makes sense. I should run. However, if I feel the same dreadful fear when my boss asks me to do a presentation at the next staff meeting, I should use my self-awareness to realize that desire to run does not make sense given the situation. Even though it may feel just as intense, I should not allow those feelings to make me run. Instead, I should recognize the feelings do not make sense, and I should decide to not run.

Pause

The instant I notice myself feeling any weird thoughts or emotions while I am interacting with someone, I must use my independent will and choose to pause. That means I must refuse to allow myself to react to what I am thinking or feeling. Sometimes, I feel a new emotion associated with my decision to pause, but I still must choose to pause.

I have studied Stephen R. Covey's work at length over the years, and here is the quote from him that started me thinking about how a simple pause (well, not always simple) could help me improve my self-control:

> *There is a gap, or a space, between stimulus*
> *and response, and the key to both our growth*
> *and happiness is how we use that space.*
> **Stephen R. Covey**
> **The 7 Habits of Highly**
> **Effective People**

The purpose of pausing is to widen that gap between a stimulus (what is going on around me) and my response to it. The wider I make that gap (the longer I pause), then the greater the chance I have of not reacting thoughtlessly to what is happening and thereby damaging my relationships.

Pausing has never been an easy thing for me to do. It has taken practice. Lots of practice. I have been working on my ability to pause for over twenty-five years, and I messed it up recently. I felt anger when Corky said something I interpreted as an insult, and I yelled at her in response. The key to a successful pause is to pause long enough to evaluate what is going on. But I yelled first, *damn it*. Of course, I apologized as soon as I took a moment to calm down, but it is always so much better when I do not react.

My ability to pause today is better than it was ten years ago. And it was better ten years ago than it was twenty years ago. It is like a muscle. The more I use it, the stronger it gets. Learning to pause has been a never-ending process of improvement for me.

Whenever I have successfully paused, that pause has given me the time I need to evaluate what is happening.

Evaluate

Once I pause, the first thing I need to evaluate is the intensity of my feelings. Using my self-awareness, I must quickly determine if my feelings are so intense I will lose control if I stay. If so, then my best chance at self-control is to walk away.

For example, when I recently yelled at Corky, it was because my anger was so intense I could not think clearly. I should have told her I would be right back and just walked away (as I have done many times before). Had I done that; I could have stayed in control.

There have been times when I found myself in situations with people where I felt an emotional reaction to something, and while I was pausing, something else happened to set off another emotional reaction.

I experience this most often when I get in an argument with someone. They say something, and I feel an emotional reaction to it. I pause. They say something else before I respond, and I feel another emotional reaction on top of the first one. If they keep talking, I can feel like I am being shot with an emotional machinegun.

Danger, Will Robinson! Abort! Walk away!

The purpose of a pause is to give myself time to evaluate what is happening. But if my emotions are so intense I cannot think clearly, then walking away is my best choice for I need to give myself time to calm down.

Of course, I should always walk away politely by saying, *Please excuse me, I'll be right back.* Or something like that.

Not all situations are that intense, of course. If I am dieting and someone offers me a piece of cake, I would not need to walk away (unless the cake looked *really* good). I should be able to evaluate with just a momentary pause by thinking if I feel the desire to eat cake while dieting, that does not make sense. If I have decided to lose weight, why would I want to eat cake? There is only one logical answer, my DNA-soup and historic baggage are pressing me to eat sweets (again).

When I was growing up, my parents frequently used food as a reward. If I was good, we might have gone out for an ice cream cone, or they might have given me a cookie. My favorite reward was, if I cleaned my plate at dinner, then I could have dessert. Basically, I would be rewarded with more food if I ate all my food. Needless to say, my historic baggage provides me with some strong feelings about food.

I did not begin to gain control of my overeating until I accepted the fact, I cannot change the past. It is completely beyond my control. Blaming anything in the past for issues I currently have does not resolve them. After all, my parents stopped feeding me in early 1972. How can they possibly be responsible for what I put in my mouth now?

However, understanding I have historic baggage that generates a strong desire to overeat does help me. I can use my self-awareness to identify when it is happening, use my independent will to pause, and then use my logic and reason to evaluate those desires.

Once I started pausing whenever I felt a physical or emotional reaction to something, I finally had discovered a way to give myself the time I needed to think. During a pause, I can evaluate both what is happening with me and what is happening around me.

For example, if I feel angry at Corky for insulting me, I try to separate my emotion from the words that triggered it. I need to evaluate if my anger makes sense or if my DNA-soup and historic baggage are reacting to something that is not actually happening to me right now. I know my wife is not prone to insulting me. So, do I truly understand what she means? The answer is usually, *no*.

If I am trying to lose weight (which I normally am), and I feel a strong desire to overeat (which I normally do), does that desire to overeat really make sense? Of course not.

After evaluating what is happening with me and those around me, I then need to use a long-term perspective to choose my best response.

Choose

Thanks to my independent will, I have the ability to choose my response in any situation. And I know if I use a long-term perspective, I can make the best choice.

Since the long-term consequences of eating cake are weight gain, joint problems, diabetes, and a poor quality of life, I know not eating cake is the better choice. I also know the long-term consequences of yelling at my wife are reduced mutual trust, a less healthy relationship, and possibly divorce if I do not get my act together. So, talking to her with respect and empathy is the better choice.

Of all these self-control steps, I always found choosing the right response to be the easiest. Pausing has been the hardest, and then responding as I have chosen to respond is probably the next hardest.

Respond

After I choose my best response, all I need to do is to respond accordingly. Yeah, that is all…

Understanding these five steps turned out to be far easier than actually doing them day-in and day-out. Situations can arise in an instant that I am not expecting. Someone might walk into a room and say something to me while I am looking away, and before I turn around my DNA-soup and historic baggage can be in full reaction mode. I have had to practice switching on my self-awareness quickly in order to spot these instantaneous reactions, and it has only been through this repeated observation of myself that I was finally able to recognize when I need to pause long enough to gain control over my responses (at least most of the time).

As I have used these five steps over the years, I have gotten better at them. But it has taken time, so I have had to be patient with myself. The most important thing to my building healthier relationships has been that I try to use these five steps whenever I interact with people.

In most situations, these five steps have been enough to enable me to exercise my self-control, but sometimes they have not been enough.

Part of my struggle with food has been that I do not like taking orders from anyone. This is a gift from my historic baggage that dates back to having been raised by a career army officer who had demanded compliance with his every order. I hated it, and I made a lot of decisions growing up that I would not put up with anyone telling me what to do.

Even though I know this, I still feel a strong emotional reaction every time I think someone is trying to give me an order. My immediate impulse is to reject it. And here is the weird part, I feel the same reaction whenever I try to tell myself what to do.

For example, if I am offered a piece of cake and use my self-awareness to realize my desire to eat it is illogical. Then, I pause long enough to evaluate what is happening, and I choose to not eat it. If I then tell myself not to eat it, I experience an immediate emotional reaction that feels something along the lines of, *You can't tell me what to do!*

How messed up is that? I experience an emotional reaction to trying to control my emotional reaction.

Historic baggage anyone?

I eventually found a solution to not being able to tell myself what to do. Rather than telling myself to not eat the cake, I change how I look at the cake. In other words, I change my perception of eating the cake.

Change Perception

I have learned that how I perceive, or interpret, something determines how I respond emotionally to it, regardless if my perception of it is accurate or not.

For example, if I see a bear charging at me in the woods, I perceive danger, and fear starts pouring from my DNA-soup. The fear then pumps adrenaline into my body which helps me run faster, and the increased speed improves my chance of survival. This fear is a good thing and makes sense. The fear/adrenaline mutation in my DNA helped my ancestors survive and enabled them to have more children than the poor non-mutants who did not feel this same level of fear or rush of adrenaline. Since the non-mutants ran slower, they ended up getting eaten by bears.

Unfortunately, if I see a solar eclipse and I think it is a sign my Sun God is angry with me, then I can feel the same fear as I would if a bear were charging at me. My fear could be even greater because there is no way I can outrun an all-powerful spiritual being.

This is how DNA-soup works. My DNA-soup responds emotionally to whatever I perceive regardless if my perception is accurate or not. The good news is, that also means I can change my emotional response to something if I change how I perceive it.

If I change my perception of the solar eclipse by under-standing it is simply the moon passing in front of the sun, then I will change my emotional response to it. I will not feel fear. Well, I might feel a little fear because it is pretty weird, but it will not be the same level of fear I felt when I thought my Sun God was angry with me.

I finally gained control over my sweet tooth by changing how I perceived sweets. Rather than telling myself to not eat cake because it made me fat, then reacting to that decision with *You can't tell me what to do*, I would look at the cake and visualize the consequences of eating it, both the short-term and long-term consequences. Basically, I stopped resisting the idea of eating the cake. Instead, I would think about eating it and how enjoyable the taste would be. Then, I would visualize getting indigestion, feeling the sugar rush and shakes, and the eventual energy crash a few hours later. I would think about the disappointment I would feel the next time I stepped on the scales, how I would feel in a year if I gained just one pound each month, and how my life would be in ten years if I were a hundred pounds heavier.

Rather than telling myself what to do, I would visualize the consequences of eating the cake until the desire to eat it went away. I would no longer want to eat the cake. So, I would not have to tell myself not to eat it.

This process takes longer than just saying *no* to myself, but it works for me when nothing else has.

If you find yourself in a similar situation where you struggle to respond in the manner you have chosen, you might want to try visualizing the consequences of the poorer choice, both the short-term and long-term consequences. Imagine those consequences and how they will make you feel until you start feeling how they will make you feel.

See if that helps.

Being Response-Able

By improving my self-control, I became what I like to refer to as *response-able*, meaning I became able to choose how I responded when I interacted with people rather than just reacting to them. This felt empowering to me because I knew how I acted now would determine how my relationships would be in the future. And if I made better choices and responded better, then my relationships would become healthier.

I had not felt in control like this before. When I was born, the quality of my life was the result of the decisions and actions of the adults around me. As I got older, even though I did not realize it, my own decisions and actions began to have a greater impact on the quality of my life. And by the time I reached twenty-five, the quality of my life and relationships was mostly the result of my own decisions and actions.

That does not mean I have not been impacted by the actions of others. Other people's actions affected me every day, and I have suffered physical and economic challenges from things other people have done. But it was how I chose to respond to those situations that had a greater impact on my life than the situations themselves.

For example, when I was laid off from the VA Hospital in 1982 due to a budget cut, I could have blamed the VA, drank away my rent money, got evicted, and moved my family into my car. Instead, I opened the yellow pages (yeah, in '82 we still used the yellow pages) and started making phone calls. Ten days later, I had a new job as a collector at a mortgage servicing company. I paid my rent and thought about what skills I needed to acquire so I would not get laid off again. I may have lost my job due to circumstances beyond my control, but I chose to do something about it I *could* control. I also realized if I had made different career choices earlier in my life, I may have been in a better situation and avoided getting laid off in the first place. Therefore, I intended to make better career choices going forward. And I have not been laid off since.

As I mentioned at the beginning of this chapter, self-control is all about recognizing what I cannot control and then focusing on what I can control. I cannot control the emotions I feel as my DNA-soup and historic baggage react to what is happening around me, but I can control how I choose to act in response to what is happening around me.

What I choose to do is always under my control. Unfortunately, there are times when I think it is easier to claim I do not have control over my choices.

For example, when I have told people things like:

> *I don't have time to do that.*
> *My wife made me come here with her.*
> *I have to be in this meeting.*
> *My boss made me do that.*

None of these statements are true because they all assume I had no choice. If I believe them, then I am hurting myself by denying control over my life. I always have a choice. I may not like any of the options that are available to me, but that does not mean I do not have a choice.

What I should have said was:

> *I choose to spend my time doing something*
>   *other than that.*
> *I chose to come here with my wife.*
> *I chose to be in this meeting.*
> *I chose to do what my boss told me to do.*

It does not matter the reason behind why I choose an option, I still choose it. It is not forced on me. I may not like the option I choose, but I can always choose the consequences of a different option if I prefer.

I can also choose to do nothing, but that is still a choice I am making.

This is what I mean by being response-able. I choose my responses, and I recognize my responses are my choice.

Besides, since my DNA-soup and historic baggage always react strongly to me thinking I am being forced to do something, the reactive noise I feel is far less when I accept it as my choice in the first place.

This is another way of changing how I perceive things. I try not to allow myself to think others are forcing me to choose a certain option. Instead, I try to be response-able and accept that I am making my own choices.

Summary

To improve my self-control, I had to learn to identify those things I could not control and separate them from those things I could control. Then I needed to focus my attention on those things I could control.

I cannot control the emotions I feel as my DNA-soup and historic baggage react to what is happening around me, but I can control how I choose to act in response to what is happening around me.

To gain control over my responses, I discovered I must follow these five steps whenever I experience physical or emotional feelings from my DNA-soup or historic baggage, especially while I am interacting with others:

1. Self-awareness – use it to recognize when my
    DNA-soup and historic baggage are generating

physical or emotional feelings to what is happening around me.

1. Pause – before I react to anything I may be feeling.
2. Evaluate – use my self-awareness during a pause to measure the intensity of my feelings and then the accuracy of my understanding of what is happening around me.
3. Choose – the best response using a long-term perspective.
4. Respond – do what I have chosen to do.

Changing how I perceive a situation changes the emotional reaction I have to it and that can improve my ability to respond in the manner I have chosen.

* * *

Before reading the next chapter, you might want to try this Self-Control Exercise:

Self-Control Exercise

1. Briefly visit someone in your life who drives you crazy.
2. Tell them you just want to know how they are.
3. Observe any emotional reactions you feel and practice pausing before you respond.
4. Evaluate if you feel you are getting close to losing control. If so, walk away immediately, but politely. If you feel in control, then take a moment and try to see the world as they see it.

5. Keep the visit brief and thank them for their time.
6. Reflect on the experience. What did you learn?

Study Group Questions

1. Why is self-awareness important to maintaining our self-control?
2. Would anyone like to share a time you paused successfully? How about a time you failed to pause?
3. How does a long-term perspective help us choose our best response?
4. Would anyone like to share a time you changed your perception of something and experienced a different reaction to it?
5. Would anyone like to share which self-control step you find to be the most difficult to practice?
6. Would anyone like to share your experience with the Self-Control Exercise?

PART TWO:

MUTUAL TRUST

<table>
<tr><td>HEALTHY RELATIONSHIPS</td></tr>
<tr><td>MUTUAL TRUST</td></tr>
<tr><td>SELF-CONTROL</td></tr>
<tr><td>LONG-TERM PERSPECTIVE</td></tr>
<tr><td>SELF-AWARENESS</td></tr>
</table>

Chapter 5

Overview

When I determined healthy relationships required mutual trust, I saw two challenges with it. The first challenge was I could not control other people. I could not *make* them trust me. The second challenge was, how would I know if a person were someone I could trust?

I felt strongly that any resolution I might find to these two challenges had to be something I *could* control, otherwise I would not be able to make it work. Eventually, I realized if I could resolve the second challenge, I would resolve the first because, if I could identify why I trusted someone, then I would also know how I should act to be worthy of someone else's trust. And how I acted was something I *could* control (or at least, I should be able to control).

I figured the easiest way to identify why I could trust someone was to identify what people did that led me to *not* trust them. Once I identified those actions, then the reason I could trust someone would be because they did not act like people I did not trust. I know this sounds like a backward approach, but it made sense to me at the time.

After much research, thought, and observation of both myself and others, I managed to narrow my list down to five general groups of actions people did that led me to not trust them. Each group included many different actions I decided were similar enough to classify together. Plus, by grouping them together, I was able to keep the list as short as possible. The five groups of actions became anyone who:

- is dishonest
- lacks integrity
- shows no compassion
- shows no empathy
- is not competent

It did not matter what they said as an explanation, I did not trust them (at least for now) because of what they did. It seemed to me whatever someone might do that would lead me to not trust them could be included in one (or more) of these five general groups of actions.

For example, I did not trust rude people. But rudeness could be caused by a lack of compassion (not caring if their rudeness bothers anyone). Or, rudeness could be caused by a lack of competence at social interaction (not knowing how to use good manners). I also did not trust unreliable people. But not being reliable could be caused by dishonesty (lying about what they intended to do), low integrity (not having their life organized enough to keep their promises), or a lack of empathy (not realizing their actions affect others).

And of course, it also made sense to me if I did any of these things, people would not trust me either. Therefore, if I did the opposite of these things, I would become more worthy of the trust of others and thereby encourage them to trust me more.

I decided to call the opposite of these general groups of actions my Trustworthy Action Groups.

The five Trustworthy Action Groups became:

- Honesty – telling the truth
- Integrity – doing what I say I am going to do
- Compassion – showing I care by doing
- Empathy – listening to understand
- Competence – doing things correctly

None of these Trustworthy Action Groups are all or nothing, meaning there are degrees of each. Based on my observations, most people are honest, at least most of the time. And most people have integrity, even though they occasionally break some of their promises. And most people have compassion and empathy toward others, although not toward everyone. And each person is competent at doing some things, but not so good at doing other things.

In addition, I do not believe anyone is perfect at doing any of these action groups all the time. I certainly am not (and I have been practicing them for decades). Everyone has room for improvement with each one.

For each person, though, I have noticed there is usually one action group in the most need of improvement. For me, it has always been empathy. I still struggle to get out of my own head and try to fully understand what is happening with other people.

Once I clarified these five trustworthy action groups, they became a yardstick I could use to measure the trustworthiness of others. Before I would trust someone even a little, I would need to observe them doing some of these five groups of actions. And the more I observed them doing these actions, the more I knew they were worthy of my trust.

As soon as I started practicing these action groups, most of the people around me started trusting me more, and the more I practiced them, the more their trust increased.

However, I have found there are some people who do not trust me regardless of how trustworthy I think I have become. I have had to remind myself I only have control over my becoming more trustworthy. I do not have control over people recognizing or responding to my improved trustworthiness. Their DNA-soup or historic baggage may be preventing them from ever trusting me, or anyone else for that matter. Unfortunately, there is nothing I can do about that, other than accept it.

In the rest of Part Two, I will take a closer look at each Trustworthy Action Group, and then in the last chapter of Part Two, I will discuss how to use them to identify who is trustworthy.

Summary

There are five Trustworthy Action Groups required for mutual trust. They are:

- Honesty – telling the truth
- Integrity – doing what I say I am going to do
- Compassion – showing I care by doing
- Empathy – listening to understand
- Competence – doing things correctly

Most people I have observed have one action group where they are most lacking. For me, it has always been empathy.

Before I trust someone, even a little, I must observe them doing some of these actions. And the more they do them, the more I know they are worthy of my trust.

Once I started practicing the five action groups, people began to trust me more than they had, and the more I did them, the more they trusted me.

Although, not everyone has trusted me just because I have become more worthy of their trust, but since I have no control over them, all I can do is accept it.

Chapter 6

Honesty

I knew if I lied, cheated, or stole, people would not trust me. Therefore, I needed to be honest with everyone with whom I wished to have a healthy relationship.

However, I realized I did not have to be honest with someone with whom I did not wish to have a relationship. If I lied to a stranger who was trying to sell me something I did not want, it never had a negative impact on my life, but it would often shorten our conversation (yay!).

Over time, I learned honesty involved more than just not lying, cheating, or stealing.

When I started my consulting business in 1992, I had read some advice that suggested I should never tell my clients I worked out of my home because it was unprofessional. They suggested I rent a post office box rather than use my home address, and if I ever needed to meet with a client, I should rent out a conference room rather than invite my client into my home. In other words, they thought I should pretend to be someone I was not.

This was referred to as, *Fake it 'till you make it.*

This advice did not sit well with me. I knew relationships that begin with a lie or misrepresentation rarely work in the long run (except in romantic comedies which are fiction), and I did not want my clients to later find out I had misrepresented myself to them in any way. So, I decided to build my business by helping clients who did not care if I worked out of my home. Besides, I figured if the president of the United States could work out of his home, how unprofessional could it be?

Since I wanted my business relationships to be healthy and last a long time, my first trustworthy action was to be honest about who I was.

In 2008, my daughter taught me there was even more to being honest than not lying, cheating, stealing, or misrepresenting myself.

Having been raised a good Catholic, I was always very careful to never tell a lie because lying was a sin, and I did not want to burn in hell for all eternity. However, I was quite good at deceiving and misleading people without *literally* telling a lie. During my five years of Catholic grammar school, no one ever told me there was anything sinful about deceiving or misleading.

For example, my mom once asked me if I had taken a cookie from the kitchen. I had, but I did not want to tell her that because she might get upset with me. And I did not want to lie to her because that would be a sin. So, I avoided answering her question by asking her if a cookie was missing. When she said *yes*, I asked her if she thought my brother or one of my sisters had taken it. That little deflection was enough to shift her attention off of me.

Based on my understanding, my not answering her question and then deflecting her attention to my siblings was not technically a lie. Therefore, I did not think it was a sin or dishonest.

In early 2008, our daughter, Melanie, helped me to understand this was not the case. I was performing at an open-mic standup comedy co-op (I was doing this because it terrified me without being dangerous), and Corky was the only one who knew what I was doing. One night when Melanie was visiting, I headed out the door to perform. She asked me where I was going. Since I felt embarrassed by what I was doing and did not want her to know, I told her I was going to a writers' group meeting. Technically, this was true because the co-op was a group of people who wrote their own material, and we met each week to evaluate each other's work (by laughing). I know, it was a stretch, but technically…

Later, when Melanie found out the truth, she got angry and said I had lied to her. When I explained I had not technically lied, she said it did not matter, it was still dishonest, and she did not trust me as much as she used to. It took me a long time to repair the damage that little (not technically a) lie had done to our relationship. Lesson learned.

Deceiving and misleading are dishonest also.

Summary

Being honest means I will not lie, cheat, or steal. But honesty is more than that. If I want to be worthy of someone's trust, I also must not deceive, mislead, or misrepresent myself to them.

* * *

Before reading the next chapter, you might want to try this Honesty Exercise:

Honesty Exercise

1. Think about a loved-one with whom you recently have not been honest.
2. List any immediate effects it had on your relationship.
3. List any long-term effects it might have on your relationship.
4. Write down your reasons for not being honest.
5. Write down how you could have handled the situation better.
6. Consider apologizing if you think doing so would improve your relationship.

Study Group Questions

1. Would anyone like to share a time when you were not honest with someone important to you?
2. What long-term consequences might result from pretending to be someone we are not?
3. Would anyone like to share your experience with the Honesty Exercise?

Chapter 7

Integrity

Acting with integrity means I keep my promises. In other words, I do what I say I am going to do.

When I did this consistently over time, people came to understand they could rely on me keeping my word. Doing what I said I was going to do built trust.

For example, if I told someone I would meet them at 10:00 AM, then I would show up at or before 10:00 AM. If I told someone I would call them the next day, then I called them the next day. Period.

As I evaluated the trustworthiness of people, I realized I had to be careful not to confuse a broken promise with a lie. I had met many honest people who did not do what they said they were going to do, even though they had every intention of keeping their promise when they made it. In other words, they were not lying to me about what they intended to do. It was just their lives lacked integrity, meaning their lives were so disorganized something would get in the way of them doing what they intended to do. They were not being dishonest, they just lacked integrity.

Keeping my promises requires me to organize my life so there is little chance something will go wrong and prevent me from doing what I say I am going to do.

Also, I must not make so many promises a glitch in my plans will prevent me from keeping one of them.

For example, when I started my consulting business, I would schedule two client appointments for each day, one in the morning at 9:00 and a second in the afternoon at 1:00. I felt this schedule would maximize my productivity. It did not work. My morning appointments frequently took longer than the amount of time I had allocated, and this created a conflict for me. I felt strongly about keeping my promises, so if I promised a client I would see them at 1:00 PM, then I wanted to be there. But I also had promised my morning client I would help them, and I felt bad about leaving to go to my afternoon appointment if we were not done yet. I ended up calling many clients with afternoon appointments to apologize and reschedule.

I eventually solved this conflict by only scheduling firm appointments in the morning. Any other appointment would be a flexible one. In other words, if a client wanted to meet at a set time, it had to be my first appointment of the day. Otherwise, we would set an appoint to be sometime after my morning appointment, whenever that might be, and I would let them know when I was on my way to their office.

I have been scheduling this way for over twenty years, and it works. My morning clients know I will stay with them if they need me, my afternoon clients are not expecting me at any set time, and I can keep my promises to both.

There are times, of course, when outside occurrences prevent me from keeping a promise. Afterall, I live in San

Diego. When the freeway traffic stops, there is no way I can make it to an appointment on time. Whenever I cannot keep a promise, I immediately contact the person to whom I gave the promise and apologize. I explain what happened and then make new arrangements. Having a cell phone has certainly made that a lot easier. I used to have to pull off the freeway and find a payphone.

I discovered apologizing whenever I could not keep a promise was especially important if I needed to break a promise with Corky or one of our children. And I soon learned I had better not let it happen again any time soon or they might begin to not trust me. And rightly so.

If I want people to trust me, they have to know I will do what I say I am going to do. Therefore, I must avoid making promises I might not be able to keep. This is also true when I promise to *not* do something.

For example, I found maintaining my integrity quite tricky when one of our children wanted to tell me a secret but did not want me to tell Corky. Or when a client's employee wanted to tell me something they did not want me to repeat to their boss (who was my client). I found my best response in these situations was to stop them from telling me. I then would explain I did not want to know because I might not be able to keep their secret, and I was unwilling to make them a promise I might not be able to keep.

As it turned out, refusing to make a promise I was unsure I could keep built just as much trust as making and keeping a promise because both demonstrated integrity.

Summary

Acting with integrity means keeping my promises as well as not making promises I am not sure I can keep. This includes not doing anything I promised I would not do.

It requires me to have my life organized well enough to ensure I can do what I say I am going to do and not do what I say I will not do.

* * *

Before reading the next chapter, you might want to try this Integrity Exercise:

Integrity Exercise

1. Think about a loved-one with whom you recently broke a promise.
2. List any immediate effects it had on your relationship.
3. List any long-term effects it might have on your relationship.
4. Write down your reasons for breaking your promise.
5. Write down how you could have handled the situation better.
6. Consider apologizing if you think doing so would improve your relationship.

Study Group Questions

1. Would anyone like to share a time when you broke a promise with someone important to you?

2. What long-term consequences might result from doing something we promised not to do?
3. Would anyone like to share your experience with the Integrity Exercise?

Chapter 8

Compassion

Whenever I feel compassion for someone, it means I care about them. And caring about someone means I care about what is best for them, not just what is best for me.

I realized compassion would help me build mutual trust because if someone knew I cared about them, then they would also know I would be looking out for their best interest, not just my own. For that to happen, of course, they would have to know I cared about them. And as it turned out, telling them was not enough. I had to show them I cared about them through my actions.

In his book, *The Seven Habits of Highly Effective People*, Stephen R. Covey talked about how love is not just a noun (defined as something I feel). It is also a verb (defined as something I do). And no, he was not talking about making love to someone, he was talking about loving someone by showing them I care about them.

Thinking about compassion as something I did rather than something I felt helped me to identify two broad groups of actions I could take to show someone I cared about them. I could show my compassion for someone by doing things *for* them, and I could show my compassion for someone by doing things *with* them.

For example, I can show Corky I love her by doing things for her like washing the dishes, taking out the trash, or doing the laundry. In addition, I can do things with her like going to the movies, playing cards, or going out to dinner.

I quickly learned, though, trying to show someone how I feel about them through my actions does not work if they misinterpret what I am doing or why I am doing it. Whatever I do to show someone my compassion has to be something they recognize and appreciate, not just something I think they *should* recognize and appreciate.

For example, when our children were young, I frequently gave them advice because I wanted to help them. Since I had learned all kinds of things during my life that I thought would help them in theirs, I figured sharing some of it with them would show them how much I loved them. As it turned out, most of the time they did not see my advice as caring. Instead, they felt like I was lecturing them. Rather than showing them how much I loved them, I was just annoying them.

It was not until I stopped giving my children advice and started listening to them that I learned what I could do that they would both appreciate and recognize as me showing them my love. Most of the time, it was just listening to them. Occasionally, they would ask for my opinion, but most often, all they wanted me to do was listen and maybe give them a hug, but without giving them any advice. They also enjoyed going out on our monthly *Dates with Dad*. We might go bowling or visit a video arcade. When Richard was thirteen, he and I went to a concert to see the *Mighty Morphin Power Rangers* (his choice, not mine).

If I never showed my compassion to my children in a way they could recognize, they may never have known how much I loved them, and they never would have trusted me. Telling them I loved them was simply not enough.

Other examples of not showing compassion would be if I tell my boss I care about my job, but I show up late, watch the clock, miss deadlines, and rush out the door at closing time. My actions would be saying I only care about being paid, not about doing my job. My boss would probably not trust me regardless how many times I might have told her my job is important to me.

Or if I tell my friend I care about him, but I make myself scarce whenever he needs my help. My actions would not be showing him I care about him, they would be showing him I only care about what I can get out of our friendship. Eventually, he probably will not trust me to be his friend anymore.

To demonstrate my compassion for someone, I must act in a way that shows them I care, and I must do it in such a way they recognize it as me caring about them.

Compassionate Priorities

When I care about someone, I want to do whatever I can to help them, even though helping them will take time and a commitment to their best interest. One of the hardest things I had to accept over the years was that I could not possibly be compassionate about everyone. I simply did not have enough time.

If I try to help feed the starving children in the world, care for the homeless in my community, help those needing emergency relief, and all the numerous other charities which I consider worthwhile, then I will not have any time left over for the people in my life I care about the most.

I certainly see nothing wrong with giving some of my time to noble causes for I have done many years of volunteer work, but I have to clarify my priorities and then focus my compassion (i.e. my time and commitment) toward those priorities that are highest on my list. I had to learn to say *no* to most things, regardless how much I may have wanted to do them, so I could say *yes* to my loved-ones.

> *It is more noble to give yourself completely to one individual than to labor diligently for the salvation of the masses.*
>
> **Dag Hammarskjöld**
> **Former Secretary-General**
> **of the United Nations**

Compassionate Mutual Benefit

I noticed when I genuinely cared about someone, I wanted to be sure they benefited from our relationship. In other words, it was important to me our relationship was mutually beneficial. And as I thought about it, I decided when the value of the benefit we each receive is greater than the time and energy we each put into our relationship, then I would consider our relationship to be healthy.

My healthiest relationships have tended to be long-term, and I believe that is because they are mutually beneficial. I still have some clients with whom I have worked for over twenty years. Corky and I have been married for over 44 years, and we have friends we have known almost that long.

If you and I both benefit from our relationship, why would we want it to end? And we will repair any damage that might be caused by momentary arguments or upsets because we value each other. When we are important to each other, we take whatever time is needed to resolve our differences.

Exception to Mutual Benefit

I found one major exception to the mutual benefit rule of relationships. When Corky became pregnant, and I was about to become a father, I realized I was about to have a brand-new parent/child relationship. How could I expect an infant to contribute to our parent/child relationship? She did, of course, just by being so damn cute, but I could not expect it.

Children must be loved unconditionally.

If I did not think I could love my child regardless of everything, then I probably should not have had one. Afterall, I could not divorce my child like a bad spouse, and I could not fire my children like bad employees.

Children must be loved and cared for no matter what, at least until they become adults. As a future father, I had to accept that responsibility before I became a parent.

When to Stop Caring and End a Relationship

To stop caring about someone and end my relationship with them was never easy, but sometimes it was necessary.

Fifteen years ago, I had a client whose business slowed down due to an economic recession. When they started to run low on cash, their solution was to pay their vendors slower. Up until that time, I had felt like we had a healthy relationship. They had valued the work I did for them, and I had valued the money they paid me.

Despite the health of our relationship, and for reasons they did not discuss with me, they began to only pay those vendors who made a lot of noise about being paid (including me). They had decided to use the old *squeaky wheel gets the grease* philosophy for paying their bills.

I have never liked pestering my clients for payment. And eventually, I began to feel this client's decision to not pay their vendors within their agreed upon terms (as well as not trying to find another solution to their cash flow problem) showed a lack of both integrity and compassion. They were not keeping their promises, and they did not appear to care enough about their vendors to discuss it with them.

When I questioned them about this change in procedure, they responded that it was what they had decided to do. They did not want to borrow money because they would have to pay interest on it, and they did not want to discuss it any further. That was when I realized they were no longer worthy of my trust. The time had come to end our relationship, so I had to stop caring about them.

I never liked ending relationships, whether they were business relationships or personal ones. I always felt sad about it and wondered if I had failed somehow. I would think to myself, *If I care about this person, then I should be able to do something to fix it!* But I came to realize that thought was just my historic baggage talking (*Only losers quit!*).

I had to accept sometimes people and circumstances can change. If I have done everything I can to be trustworthy, and I am convinced our relationship will never return to one of mutual trust and mutual benefit, then I need to stop caring and end it. And once I am convinced a relationship needs to end, I also know I need to end it as soon as possible.

There was a time when I would allow unhealthy relationships to continue. The problem was, the longer I stayed stuck in an unhealthy relationship, the longer it was before I could focus on building new, healthier relationships.

I eventually developed a way I could identify potentially unhealthy relationships. What I did was to imagine I owned a magic wand (I know it sounds silly but bear with me). If I touched someone with this magic wand, they would disappear from my life. No one would be hurt; they would just be transported to a new life someplace else. Then, I would ask myself if there was anyone in my life I might want to touch with my magic wand. If I thought there was, then I knew I needed to evaluate my relationship with that person.

First, I would ask myself if they were worthy of my trust. If they were, then I would ask myself if our relationship was healthy and mutually beneficial (i.e. were we both receiving more benefit from our relationship than the value of the time and energy we put into it)? And finally, I would ask myself if there was anything I could do to fix it?

By asking myself these three questions, I was able to make better decisions about my relationships because I had a clearer understanding of them. This clarity then enabled me to act, regardless of whether I decided to try and fix a relationship, or I decided to end it.

There was another business relationship I ended that I want to mention, but this one was different in that we were both still benefiting from our relationship, and I still felt like my client was trustworthy. The problem with this relationship was I did not feel like my client would continue to benefit if our relationship continued. I did not need to stop caring and end our relationship; I needed to end our relationship because I cared. Here is what happened.

I had been working for this client as a part-time Chief Financial Officer (CFO) for over three years while her business grew from $50,000 in annual sales to over $5.5 million. Shortly thereafter, the company's sales surpassed a million dollars in one month, and I knew my client needed a full-time CFO. I had already been struggling to keep up with the work she needed, and the company just kept growing.

When I explained this to her, she asked me to come onboard full-time. I told her I could not because I was not willing to abandon all my other clients, and there was no way I could handle all their work while trying to keep up with what she needed. I told her it was in her best interest if we found a full-time replacement for me.

She hated the idea of me leaving, and we argued about it for months. But when the company's sales exceeded a million dollars in one week, she finally agreed. So, we worked together to find a replacement, and I worked with her new CFO for a year to help with the transition.

I ended this business relationship because it was in the best interest of my client. I knew she needed more than I could provide, even though she did not see it.

Although we ended our business relationship, we are still friends to this day.

Summary

Compassion is caring about people. If someone knows I care about them, then they also know I will look out for their best interest, not just my own. And that knowledge builds trust.

However, for someone to know I care about them, I must show it to them through my actions and in such a way they recognize and appreciate.

Because compassion requires time and a commitment to another, I have to limit who I care about in order to ensure I have enough time left for my loved-ones.

When I care about someone, I want them to benefit from our relationship. When we both benefit, our relationship tends to last a long time.

The one exception to the mutual benefit rule is my relationships with my children. I cannot expect my children to contribute to our relationship, and I needed to accept that before I became a parent.

If I have an unhealthy relationship which I cannot fix, it is best if I stop caring about that person and end our relationship as soon as possible. Sometimes, however, I found ending a relationship was in the best interest of the other person. Even then, it is best if I end it as soon as possible.

*   *   *

Before reading the next chapter, you might want to try this Compassion Exercise:

Compassion Exercise

1. Think about someone you care about and make a list of the benefits you receive from that relationship.
2. How grateful are you for this relationship?
3. Make a list of the benefits you think they receive from your relationship.
4. Ask them what they see are the benefits they receive from your relationship.
5. How well does your list match theirs?
6. Discuss with them what they think you could do *for* them as well as what you could do *with* them that would increase the benefit they receive from your relationship.
7. Do those things.

Study Group Questions

1. What can we do *for* our loved-ones to show them we care about them?
2. What can we do *with* our loved-ones to show them we care about them?
3. Would anyone like to share a decision you made to end a relationship? What were your reasons?
4. How can we improve the benefits we receive from each other during these meetings?
5. Would anyone like to share your experience with the Compassion Exercise?

<u>*Chapter 9*</u>

Empathy

Having empathy for someone means I try to understand them so completely I can imagine experiencing the world as they experience it. I want to understand what they think, how they feel, and why they are doing what they are doing. If I can experience it deeply enough, then they may recognize I understand them.

In 1988, the mortgage servicing company where I worked sent me to a class called *The 7 Basic Habits of Highly Effective People*. This class was based on the research of Stephen R. Covey (I have already used quotes from his best-selling book which was published the following year).

At the time of this *7 Basic Habits* class, my relationship with Corky was strained. Our son, Richard, was six and had been diagnosed with Attention Deficit Hyperactivity Disorder (ADHD), and Corky and I were wrestling with how to handle him. He was struggling in school and in life, and none of the parenting skills we had used so successfully with our daughter, Melanie, worked with Richard.

I researched ADHD and did not understand why it was such a problem since I had experienced many of the same symptoms growing up. So, Corky and I started attending support groups. We went to counseling, and we met regularly with Richard's teachers. Nothing worked. Corky and I were both frustrated, and so was Richard. On top of that, our finances were tight even though we both worked. Our available time was limited, our stress level was high, and our patience was thin.

In the *7 Basic Habits* class, I studied the first four habits and found them all interesting, but not so unique they did not feel somewhat similar to books I had previously studied. Then, I reached habit number five:

> *Seek First to Understand,*
> *Then to be Understood.*

Covey explained the difference between me projecting my viewpoint on others rather than me listening and trying to understand their viewpoint.

For example, Richard once told me about a problem he was having with his homework. His story reminded me of a time when I was about his age and had a similar problem with my homework. I then assumed he was experiencing the same thing. Since I was projecting my viewpoint onto him, I thought I understood him. Unfortunately, he did not agree.

According to Covey, just because I understood what had happened with me did not mean I understood what was happening with my son.

As I thought about it, I realized I had always tended to project my thoughts, feelings, and motivations onto other people rather than trying to understand theirs. Since I was convinced I understood them, I tried to help them understand their situation by explaining what had happened to me. I rarely could get anyone to see my viewpoint. In fact, all my life, I had found it frustrating to try and get people to understand me.

That was when a lightbulb went off in my head. I had no control over people. I could not force them to understand me regardless of how many times I may have tried. So, rather than be frustrated by trying to change someone's viewpoint I could not control, I needed to focus my attention on changing someone's viewpoint I could control, which was mine. I needed to work on improving *my* ability to understand *them*.

Afterall, since I had always felt better when someone had tried to understand me, it made sense I could make other people feel better if I tried to understand them. And if I could understand them well enough that they recognized I understood them, then perhaps they would be willing to try and understand me.

Once I decided to try and understand my son better, I had to start listening to him and stop relating my experiences to his. I needed to try and understand what was going on with him from his perspective, not mine. In other words, I needed to be more empathetic.

The first time I tried this with Richard, I found I needed to use my imagination and think about what it would be like to have his life, his opinions, his thoughts, his emotions, his motivation, and his dreams. I did not necessarily agree with him, I was just trying to understand him from his viewpoint. Over time, as I understood him better, we began to build a stronger bond of trust between us, and our relationship improved dramatically. I even began to suspect he may have inherited his ADHD from me, which did not make me feel very good.

As I applied this habit in my other relationships, I spent more time trying to understand others and less time being frustrated by trying to get them to understand me. And all my relationships improved. In fact, many of my relationships improved the moment I simply *tried* to better understand them, even when I did not do it very well.

Just like all the other actions I have discussed, empathy has taken me a lot of time and practice to develop. And it has been far easier for me to understand this habit than it has been for me to do it. In fact, I still struggle with it today. But the most important thing I have found about this habit is I at least try to be empathetic whenever I interact with people. I have never reached a complete understanding of any of the people in my life, but when I have understood them better, our relationships have improved.

Compassion versus Empathy

I started writing this book in the spring of 2018 and have been working on it now for over six months. Although it has been almost thirty years since that lightbulb went off in my head, I realize there are still times when I completely disregard empathy. As it turns out, I appear to have a rather delicate balance between my compassion for people and my empathy for them. Sometimes I allow my compassion for someone to push my empathy aside.

For example, I met with a client recently who told me she was hiding a large amount of cash in her closet at home. No, she is not a drug dealer. She sells her products at farmers' markets, and most of her customers pay her in cash.

When I explained to her that she was taking an unnecessary risk by keeping all that money in cash, she told me she did not trust banks.

I was so concerned about her losing her money, I did not try to understand her viewpoint. Rather, I allowed my compassion to overwhelm my empathy. I told her she should not take that kind of risk, and if her money were ever stolen, or lost in a fire, she would be devastated. Besides, not trusting a bank to keep her money safe was not logical and she should not allow her emotions to control her decision. I even considered threatening to drop her as a client as a way of pressuring her into taking my advice and depositing the cash into her bank account. Basically, I was trying to badger her into doing what I thought she should do.

And of course, it did not work.

That evening, when I told Corky about my meeting, she pointed out I had not been very empathetic to my client. She was right, of course, so I analyzed why I had behaved so poorly and that was when I realized I had allowed my compassion to overwhelm my empathy.

The next time I saw this client, I apologized to her for my behavior and asked her to forgive me. I explained my personal revelation about letting my compassion overwhelm my empathy. She had already known I cared about her, and that knowledge had made it all the harder for her to experience my badgering behavior.

After I explained it, she understood and forgave me.

She also realized she struggled with the same conflict between compassion and empathy with her children. She loved them so much, she just wanted them to do what she told them to do so they would be safe.

I told her I had that same struggle as a parent.

The Problem with *The Golden Rule*

As a child, I was taught *The Golden Rule*, meaning I should treat people the same way as I want them to treat me. It made sense at the time.

The problem with *The Golden Rule* is it does not always work. Some people do not want me to treat them the same way as I want them to treat me.

What I have found that works every time is to learn how someone wants me to treat them (use my empathy), and then treat them like that and not assume they want me to treat them the same way as I want them to treat me.

Consequences of No Empathy

I am sorry to say, there have been many times in my life when I had little or no empathy for other people, and I have suffered the consequences of ruined relationships because of it. I am going to share with you an example out of my past. It is an embarrassing story which my wife would prefer I leave out of this book, but I believe it illustrates exactly what can happen when someone (in this case me) does not use empathy in their relationships.

In fact, it was my later analysis of what I had done wrong at that time which led me to investigate what I needed to do to improve my self-control.

In 1992, I was a partner in a real estate research and consulting firm. My five partners were all real estate gurus while I was the sole business guy. Each of my partners was responsible for the research and consulting of a different geographic area. As a company, we covered all of Southern California as well as southern Nevada. I was responsible for support services, including Accounting and Finance.

My partners and I did not get along. I wanted us to build a company that would profitably expand across the United States. They wanted higher salaries and company cars.

My staff and I shared office space in San Diego with the partner in charge of the San Diego region and his staff. The San Diego partner and I could barely stand each other, partly because both our wives worked at the company. His wife was the office manager whose primary job was answering the phones and ordering supplies. Corky was the Controller whose primary job was to ensure our customers paid us, our venders were paid on time, and the partners had accurate financial reports so we could make better business decisions.

My partner's wife did not like that Corky was paid more money than she was. Since all the partners had identical salaries, I suppose she probably thought all the partners' wives should have identical salaries too.

Another reason my partner and I did not get along was that my partner treated my staff as if they worked for him. He would not hesitate to tell my Accounts Payable (A/P) clerk to answer the phones whenever he wanted to take his wife to lunch, regardless of what other higher priority tasks my A/P clerk may have had to do.

Of course, the real reason I did not get along with my partner was because I never tried to understand him. I only demanded he change his behavior, which he would not. And this was almost four years after I had learned to *Seek first to understand, then to be understood* (and obviously, I was still struggling to apply it in my life).

The day before I was going to leave on vacation, my partner once again told my A/P clerk to cover the phones, and I flew into a rage.

Keep in mind, this was years before I had identified the five steps for self-control. I was self-aware enough to know I was angry, but I did not pause at all or evaluate the situation from a long-term perspective. Instead, I stormed into his office, slammed the door, and once again demanded he stop telling my staff what to do. If he wanted someone to cover the phones, he could damn well ask me for my staff's help or answer them himself.

He stated he was the head of the office, and he could do whatever he wanted to do with the staff. I told him he was full of shit. At which point, our voices quickly rose above the decibels of a rock concert.

That was when my partner's wife burst into the room.

I was still standing by the door, and she started shouting at me that I had no right to yell at her husband. I told her to get out, gently pushed her back out the door, and slammed it shut again. She tried to force her way back in, but I blocked the door with my foot.

My partner then came charging around his desk yelling at me to keep my hands off his wife. I thought for sure he was going to punch me in the face, but he just pushed me aside, opened the door, and ushered his wife out of the office.

I was shaking from the adrenaline but managed to walk back to my own office. After a few minutes, I calmed down enough to get back to work.

Four hours later, my partner's wife walked into my office with two police officers and said she was putting me under citizen's arrest for battery. One officer told me to stand, and he cuffed my hands behind my back while the other officer asked me to accompany them to their squad car so we could discuss what happened. Not wanting to be paraded through the office in handcuffs, I asked the officers if we could perhaps just have a seat here in my office and discuss it. They agreed, and my partner's wife left.

After twenty minutes of discussion, the police officers removed the handcuffs and told me to contact the District Attorney's office when I returned from vacation to find out if there would be any further action taken.

A week later, after returning home from a distracted visit to Disney World with my family, I found a letter from my managing partner asking me to stay home until further notice.

He said he and the other partners had to figure out what to do. When I met with the District Attorney, he told me to stay away from my partner's wife. If there was no further trouble, then my record would be expunged in six months.

My partner's wife never filed charges.

Two months later, my partners terminated my employment. They also bought out my partnership interest for less than ten percent of its value, citing a clause in our partnership agreement. I was devastated and sank into a depression.

A few weeks later, they forced Corky out. That worsened how I felt. How could they do this to us? Corky and I had all our financial eggs in that one basket, and my partners had erased everything we had spent three years helping to build. I could not believe they would do that to us, and I moped around the house for weeks feeling sorry for myself.

I did not start feeling better until I stopped blaming my partners for the mess my family was in. Once I started analyzing what *I* had done that resulted in our situation, I finally began to feel better. I was the one who had argued with my partners. I was the one who never tried to understand them. And I was the one who had charged into my partner's office and yelled at him.

I could have acted better. I could have acted sooner.

I could have tried to be more empathetic.

I did not blame myself for what had happened. I just recognized my responsibility for it. And the reason that made me feel better was because if I was the one who had caused it to happen, then I could prevent it from happening again in the future. That realization brought the incident back into the realm of what I could control. I just needed to forgive myself for my mistake and change my behavior going forward.

Not that I could fix the relationships with my partners, they were irreparably damaged. But I could take better care of any business relationships I might build in the future.

Much of this book resulted from my analyzing what I did wrong with my partners. I wish I did not have to experience that day to understand all this, but since I cannot go back in time and give myself a copy of this book, I can only hope it finds its way into the hands of people who might learn how to avoid some of the mistakes I have made. This one being the biggest. And I am happy to say, I have not done anything quite that stupid since.

Summary

Empathy is striving to understand someone so completely they realize I understand them and I can imagine experiencing the world just as they experience it.

Since I cannot control people, I cannot force them to understand me. Therefore, I need to focus my attention on the one person I can control, myself, and practice trying to better understand others. Once people recognize I do understand them, then they just might feel comfortable enough to try and understand me.

* * *

Before reading the next chapter, you might want to try this Empathy Exercise:

Empathy Exercise

1. Think about someone you know who does not trust you, but you wish they would.
2. Evaluate your actions toward them. Can you recall a time you demonstrated a lack of empathy?
3. How could you have handled the situation better?
4. To repair the relationship, try apologizing to them for how you acted.
5. Then explain you are trying to become a better version of yourself and you will try harder to understand them in the future.
6. Ask them what *they* would appreciate you doing for them or with them.
7. Make a list of what they would appreciate.
8. Do one of the things on the list.
9. Wait awhile (but not longer than a couple of days) and do another one.
10. As you interact with them, listen to them empathetically. Try to experience the world as they do. Be polite and respectful.
11. Update your list of things you could do for them or with them based on your interactions.
12. Repeat steps 8-12 until they trust you or they convince you they never will.

Study Group Questions

1. Why should we try to understand someone before we try to be understood by them?

2. Would anyone like to share a time you struggled to understand someone?
3. Would anyone like to share a time you struggled to be understood by someone?
4. How can we improve our empathy with each other during these meetings?
5. Would anyone like to share your experience with the Empathy Exercise?

Chapter 10

Competence

To me, competence is having the ability to achieve a successful outcome when doing a repetitive activity. In other words, having the skills needed to consistently do a task well, over and over again.

For example, if I want to be a competent dentist that people will trust, then I must be able to clean their teeth regularly without leaving any tartar behind or damaging anyone's mouth. And if I want to be a competent friend, then I must be able to relate to my friend whether they are having a good day or a bad one.

As I thought about competence, I realized I would need to be competent in two distinctive groups of activities before people would trust me:

- Social activity
- Work-related activity

Without social skills, people would struggle to relate to me, and I would run the constant risk of doing or saying something they might think was rude. Since I did not trust rude people, I did not want others to think I was rude.

Without work-related skills, no one would trust me to do a job-related task. Which made sense to me since I would not trust anyone to do a job if I thought they lacked the skills to do it well.

Social Activity

If I wanted people to trust me, I had to interact with them without them feeling like I was being rude. That required me to exercise both my self-awareness and my empathy. I would need to stay self-aware enough to monitor my behavior and how people reacted to my behavior. Then, I would need to be empathetic enough to the people around me to recognize when I needed to adjust my behavior for them.

I found two sets of social skills that helped me with social interactions. To work, however, I had to stay both self-aware and empathetic while I used them. They are:

- Good manners – to avoid being rude
- Empathetic communication – so we can understand each other

Whenever I practiced both good manners and empathetic communication, my social interactions were better.

Good Manners

Good manners are socially acceptable behaviors that reduce the likelihood of me being rude to someone.

I do not mean the stilted manners they teach in finishing school, like only skimming my spoon across the surface of my soup in the direction that is away from me. No, I mean empathetic manners, meaning I try to behave around other people in a way I think they will appreciate. And since different people appreciate different manners, I adjust my behavior for whoever happens to be around me.

For example, my manners with my loved-ones are more relaxed than my manners with strangers. I act one way at home with my family but then act differently if we are in a restaurant. That is because the strangers sitting at the tables around us in the restaurant might take offense to my behavior if I act the same way as I do when I am at home with my family without any strangers around.

I am not trying to pretend to be a different person. I am simply adjusting my behavior to avoid being rude to people. I am still being myself, just a more polite version of myself when the situation calls for it.

Since people will trust me more if they do not think I am rude, when in doubt, I try to be polite. And if I do or say something that upsets someone, I politely apologize and adjust my behavior so it will not happen again.

I compiled a list of words and phrases I felt helped improve my manners. I try to use them as often as possible:

- *Hi.* or *Hello.* – I try to be friendly
- *Please.* and *Thank you.* – I seldom feel like I use these words as often as I should
- *Excuse me.* – before I interrupt someone or push my way past them in a crowd
- *What do you think?* – when I sincerely want to know, and I practice sincerely wanting to know
- *I love you.* – when it is true and appropriate

In other words, I try to be kind, courteous, and nice. But only when I mean it. Pretending to be kind, courteous, and nice does not feel right to me. So, when I find it difficult to be sincerely kind, courteous, and nice to someone, then I try to avoid that person.

Unfortunately, there are times when I cannot avoid someone I consider to be difficult to get along with. When that happens, I do my best to try and listen to understand them. What I have discovered about listening to understand someone I consider to be difficult is that frequently, the better I understand them empathetically, the more I sincerely want to be kind, courteous, and nice to them.

When that does not work, however, I just make plans to change my life so I can avoid them in the future.

Empathetic Communication

I knew my ability to communicate had been an essential skill for me to use in establishing and maintaining all my healthy relationships. I also knew my inability to communicate had been a contributing factor in my failure to establish and maintain many of my previous relationships.

How many times had I felt like someone did not understand what I was trying to say? How many times had I struggled to understand what someone was trying to tell me? Why was it so hard? I suspected it was because I did not know how to communicate very well.

I decided I needed to learn more about communication.

I had read communication was simply the transfer of ideas or thoughts from one person to another. Sounded simple enough. And yet, every argument I ever had resulted primarily from a breakdown of communication. I had either not transferred my ideas and thoughts to the other person effectively, or I had not understood their ideas and thoughts correctly, or I was trying to communicate with them when they were not interested in communicating with me.

I realized communication had broken down every time I had stopped trying to understand the other person and focused entirely on being understood. If someone failed to understand me, I often tried talking louder, or I might have tried to manipulate or badger them so I could *win* the conversation. And every time I tried to win a conversation, all I ever succeeded in doing was damaging my relationship with them.

As it turned out, communication was not simple at all. It required both effort and focus.

With continued research, I discovered what I needed to do to communicate effectively. I had to improve my ability to do these two things:

- Empathetic listening – duplicating the thoughts and ideas of others from their viewpoint
- Empathetic talking – enable others to duplicate my thoughts and ideas from their viewpoint

Of the two, I found my need to listen to be the most important and (sadly) the least practiced. Most of the time, I did not want to listen to someone until I felt like they had heard and understood me first. Once I realized I could not *make* someone listen to me, I knew the only thing I had under my control was listening to them.

So, I started listening to people with the intention of understanding them, and I found they would reach a point where they felt like I did understand them. And once they felt like I understood them, frequently they would become willing to listen to me.

That was how I finally worked out the best way I could communicate within the realm of what I could control.

Empathetic Listening

I define empathetic listening as striving to fully understand the person who is talking. Not just what they say, but why they say it, how they feel about it, and how they view it.

I have read there are many different ways to listen to someone, and the best method to use depends on the circumstances. Here are a few of the ways I found.

If I were a lawyer listening to a witness I was about to cross-examine in court, I should be *listening to refute* what they are saying.

If I were a doctor listening to a patient describe their pain, I should be *listening to diagnose* their problem by relating what they say to my medical knowledge.

And if I were lost and asking someone for directions, I should be *listening to follow* their instructions.

I determined these different types of listening, however, could damage a relationship if I used them when I should be listening to understand someone.

Imagine what would happen if my daughter were telling me about an upset she had while on a date, and I listened to refute what she was saying and then cross-examined her. Or, imagine what would happen if I listened to diagnose her upset and then provided suggestions on how to fix it.

I had tried both, and neither one worked.

If I am going to try and listen to someone with whom I wish to build a healthy relationship, empathetic listening has to be my gold standard.

Empathetic listening requires me to do the following:

- Be there
- Focus my attention on them
- Try to see the world as they see it
- Ask for clarification as needed
- Check with them to see if I understand
- Ask if they are interested in my viewpoint

Being there sounds easy, but I found it to be much harder than I thought. It requires me to bring all my awareness into the here and now. I have to set aside all the distractions and noise in my head and be in the present. And I cannot allow my DNA-soup or historic baggage to divert my attention to perceived conflicts or past upsets.

Just for fun, try closing your eyes for a moment and listen to the noise in your head. You might start questioning why you are sitting here with your eyes closed, or you might hear a song playing, or you might have a thought about something you need to do, or you might remember a problem you have been trying to solve.

Go ahead. Give it a try. I will wait.

When I first tried this, I found my head was full of stuff to distract me. But if I wanted to try and listen to someone empathetically, I needed to master setting aside all those distractions and just be in the here and now.

How did I do that? Practice, practice, practice.

My first attempt at being in the here and now happened in 1973. I was in the barracks at March Air Force Base outside Riverside, California and was reading a book on Gestalt therapy. Following the author's instructions, I lay down on my cot and focused on my breathing. By concentrating on the air going in to inflate my lungs and then going out as my lungs deflated, the noise in my head gradually quieted.

I think it took close to an hour that first time. Now that I think back on it, I may even have fallen asleep. But I kept practicing, and some months later, I felt in much better control of my attention.

Since then, I have taken other classes that were designed to help me focus. I practiced the communication training routines they taught in Scientology. Since leaving there, I tried meditation, and more recently, I learned yoga. In my experience, they all worked in some capacity.

I still do my own version of yoga every night before bed. I find it helpful to quiet my mind so I can fall asleep.

To me, the most important thing is I found something that worked for me because if I could not quiet the distractions in my head, then focusing on someone else empathetically would be almost impossible.

As I improved my ability to quiet the noise in my head and be in the here and now, I was then able to better focus my attention on whoever was talking to me so I could listen to them empathetically.

Focusing on them is not easy either. It requires me to not do or think about anything other than listening to them. I found even after I quiet the noise in my head, it still takes constant effort to stay focused. After all, someone is talking to me, and what they say reminds me of other things. So, I have to exercise my self-control, keep the noise in my head quiet, and continue to focus my attention on them.

I came to realize trying to multi-task is a bad idea. I have never seen anyone do more than one thing at a time and do them well (including me). However, I have seen many people try to do more than one thing at a time and do them all poorly (also including me). This especially applies to communication. If I try to listen to someone while reading a text from someone else, I am not focusing my attention on either one of them empathetically.

For example, there were times when Corky and I would have sensitive conversations in our car while I was driving. When this first happened, I tried to shift my focus from my driving to our conversation. After a few close calls with accidents, I realized that was a bad idea. I then kept my primary focus on driving and allocated what attention I had left to our conversations. After a few upsets and arguments, I realized that was a bad idea also. I finally realized if we had something sensitive to discuss, I needed to ask her if we could wait and talk about it later when I could give her my full attention. That worked much better. However, it was critical we actually did discuss whatever it was as soon as I parked the car, otherwise she might have felt like I was trying to use my driving as an excuse to dodge the conversation.

I have struggled to focus my attention all my life which is why I suspected our son probably inherited his ADHD from me. When someone starts talking to me, I must force myself to shift my attention to them. I find this especially difficult when I am absorbed in something. The interruption is jarring. Sometimes, I have to ask the person to please repeat what they said to me first because my attention was still on what I was doing and not on what they were saying.

While I am listening to someone, I occasionally catch myself judging their communication skills. When this happens, I have to remind myself judging the speaker is not listening empathetically, even if I am only evaluating how well the speaker is talking.

I frequently have to remind myself I am trying to see the world from the other person's viewpoint. That means I must put my viewpoints aside. I must put my critical thinking aside. I must put my own experiences aside. I do not want to judge, critique, or interrogate. I just want to try and understand their viewpoint from *their* viewpoint.

While I do that, I also have to remind myself I am not trying to solve their problem, fix their understanding, change their mind, or help them in any way. Nor am I trying to think of similar situations from my life I can share with them. I am only trying to understand them, and to do that, I must accept whatever they are telling me as the way they see things right now. I do not have to agree with what they are telling me. I just have to accept it as their viewpoint and try to understand it from their viewpoint.

I find this particularly difficult when the person talking to me is criticizing me for something.

For example, a few years back, I had a client who thought I had entered a check into QuickBooks incorrectly. When I showed her how I had entered it was correct, she insisted it should be different.

Rather than argue with her (which I felt like doing), I maintained my self-awareness, fought the urge to defend myself, and continued listening to understand her viewpoint. When I finally understood her fully, I realized she was trying to tell me she thought the check should have been entered on a different screen. When I showed her that how I had entered the check had the same result as entering it on the other screen, she agreed it was fine.

While I listen to people, I use my imagination to try and see the world as they see it. If I cannot, I need to ask them for clarification. But I must be careful not to ask questions for any other purpose than clarification.

For example, if I am talking with my daughter about her upset during a date, it is okay to ask, "I'm sorry, but I'm not quite following. What do you mean when you say John acted aggressively?" However, it is not okay to ask, "Why on earth would you ever go out with John?" The first question asks her for clarification while the second question implies a critical judgment of her actions. The first question encourages further communication. The second question discourages it.

Since I do not like talking to people who judge me while I am talking to them, I suspect people do not like talking to me if I judge them while they are talking to me.

Once I reach a point where I feel like I understand what someone is trying to tell me, and I also feel like I understand how they feel about it, then I check with them to see if I am correct in both areas.

For example, I would say something to my daughter like, "So, you're angry because John tried to kiss you."

If my daughter then tells me I do understand her correctly, she says she is done talking about it, and she says she is interested in hearing what I have to say about it, only then is it okay for me to express my viewpoint.

One of my biggest struggles with empathetic listening has been when I have an idea I think will help the person who is talking to me, perhaps to clarify what they are saying or maybe to correct a misunderstanding. When my desire to help is coupled with my personal worry I will forget what I want to say, my inclination is to interrupt them so I can insert my comment.

I have a client with similar tendencies. We used to interrupt each other frequently, and each interruption led us down a tangent resulting in long, unproductive conversations. The only workable solution I found was to force myself to be quiet. I had to stop myself from thinking about things I wanted to say because that was not listening empathetically. And I had to accept the notion that anything I might forget to say later was not as important as my empathetic listening.

Here is a list of some of the things I discovered I need to *avoid* doing when listening empathetically:

- Pretending to listen (while I do something else)
- Selectively listening (while I do something else)
- Listening just long enough to decide what I want to say in response
- Judging
- Criticizing
- Finding fault
- Trying to figure out how to change their mind
- Trying to figure out how to solve their problem
- Trying to figure out how to teach them what I think they need to know
- Thinking about similar experiences I had and what I learned from them
- Making them feel uncomfortable by asking probing questions rather than clarifying questions (interrogating)

If I do any of the above, I am not listening empathetically. And it has taken me a lot of practice to stop doing them (most of the time). And I mean lots and lots of practice.

After all these years, I still have plenty of room for improvement, but the better I have gotten, the healthier my relationships have become.

I also have noticed I talk a lot less than I used to.

Empathetic Talking

Empathetic talking is striving to be fully understood by the person to whom I am talking, not just what I am saying, but why I am saying it, how I feel about it, and maybe even how I see the world. It is my gold standard of talking for the purpose of building healthy relationships.

I do not expect anyone to whom I am talking to understand my viewpoint from *my* viewpoint. I figure that is unrealistic. And of course, I have no control over how they listen to me, anyway. However, getting someone to understand my viewpoint from *their* viewpoint is realistic.

Empathetic talking requires me to do the following:

- Be there
- Focus my attention on them
- Get their attention
- Explain my viewpoint in such a way they can understand it
- Ask if they need clarification
- Check with them to see if they understand
- Ask for their opinion about what I said

Being there and focusing on them is still not easy. While I explain my viewpoint, I have to continue to exercise my self-control, keep the noise in my head quiet, and focus my attention on the person to whom I am talking.

And of course, I need to get their attention before I say anything important. If someone is not listening to me, there is no use in talking to them other than to get their attention. So, if they are preoccupied with something or just not willing to talk to me, I ask them if there is another time we can talk. I try to be empathetic to what is happening with them and not try to explain my viewpoint unless they are ready and willing to listen.

While talking to someone, I constantly have to remind myself my only purpose is to get them to understand my viewpoint. I am not trying to lecture them, or convince them I am right, or impress them with how I see things. I also have to remember to be patient and use familiar language, avoiding jargon they may not understand. I want to use examples that make sense to them, not just to me. And I want to avoid debating with them or trying to be clever. And on top of all that, I need to pay attention to them to ensure they are understanding me. Because if they are struggling to understand what I am saying, I need to stop talking and start empathizing with their struggle and try to find another way to explain my idea so they *can* understand it.

And of course, I need to avoid judging the listening skills of the person to whom I am talking for I cannot expect them to listen to me empathetically.

Sometimes when I talk to people, their attention drifts away. This is why I need to focus my attention on them while

I talk. If I notice a blank look on their face and they start nodding their head mechanically, I know I have lost them and there is no use continuing to talk. I must stop and ask them empathetically if they need clarification, or do they have something they want to say, or is there something else on their mind.

Whenever I notice someone reacting emotionally to something I am saying, I also need to stop talking since they probably have stopped listening. If I want them to start listening again, I need to ask them what is happening and listen empathetically until I understand why they are emotional. Only after they realize I understand their feelings can their willingness to listen to me return.

When I first started doing this, I felt like it was unfair. Why did I always have to be the one to listen empathetically when the person I was talking to did not have to listen empathetically to me? The reason was simple. I have no control over them. I only have control over how I communicate with them, both talking and listening.

Therefore, empathetic talking had to be defined as me staying focused on them and striving to achieve their understanding of my viewpoint. And the only way I can do that is to talk only when I have their attention and their willingness to listen. If I do not have their attention or their willingness to listen, I must switch back to empathetic listening until I understand why they are not listening. It is only through my empathetic listening to them that they can get to a point where they feel like I understand them. And it is only after they reach that point will they be willing to listen to me.

If they are not willing to listen to me for whatever reason, then the conversation has to be over, at least for now. I never have been successful at trying to force anyone to understand my viewpoint when they were not interested in listening to me, regardless how many times I tried.

Once we get to the point where I feel they have understood my viewpoint, then I switch back to empathetic listening and ask them if they understand it and what they think about it. As they talk to me about what I said, I try to understand their understanding of my viewpoint from their viewpoint. Is their understanding what I am trying to say?

Empathetic talking is trying to get someone to understand my viewpoint from *their* viewpoint. Even if they do not agree with my viewpoint, they can still understand it. We can always agree to disagree, but only if we both understand each other first. There have been times when I have argued with people, even to the point of frustration and anger, only to discover in the end we had agreed all along. We both had been trying to say the same thing, just in different ways. Of course, this has only happened when I insisted on them understanding me before I tried to understand them.

I have probably tried just about every possible wrong way to talk to people. This has been the only one I ever found that has worked consistently.

Through this process of empathetic listening and then empathetic talking, I have improved the mutual trust with the people in my life, and that has strengthened the health of our relationships. This strengthening happened even when the person I was talking with was not communicating with me empathetically. When they were, it was even better.

Work-Related Activity

Work-related skills are essential if I want someone to trust me enough to do a job because without the necessary skills, I cannot do the job consistently well.

When I reassessed my work-life back in 1980 because Corky was pregnant, I knew I could not support our family on the tiny amount of money I made in Scientology. I also knew I did not have the work-related skills I would need to land a decent paying job. So, after I quit, I took the only job I could find. I became a mortgage broker for a friend of mine. I also studied at night to get my real estate license because my friend could not pay me until I had one.

Once I had my real estate license, I went back to college at night to study real estate so I could better understand what I was doing. This improved my work-related skills, plus the monthly check from the GI Bill helped us financially.

When the economy went into a recession at the end of 1980, the prime interest rate hit 21.5% and my mortgage business started shrinking. By 1982, I was doing more mortgage collection work than funding new mortgages and my commissions had all but dried up. We were struggling to pay our bills and saw no end in sight. So, I shut the business down, and we moved to San Diego where I took a job as a janitor at the VA hospital. Despite having become one of their best janitors, I was laid off three months later due to a budget cut and no seniority.

Ten days after being laid off, my mortgage collections experience helped me get a job at the mortgage servicing company as a collector. I also went back to college at night to get a degree in business. If I wanted a stable career, I knew I had to increase my work-related skills.

No matter what career path I have been on (and there have been many), I have made every effort to develop the skills I needed to be the best I could be at what I was doing. Not only has it helped me improve my relationships with my co-workers, but it has also increased my income.

> *If a man is called to be a street sweeper, he should sweep streets even as Michelangelo painted, or Beethoven composed music, or Shakespeare wrote poetry. He should sweep streets so well that all the hosts of heaven and earth will pause to say, here lived a great street sweeper who did his job well.*
>
> **Dr. Martin Luther King, Jr.**
> **Leader of the American**
> **Civil Rights Movement**

Work-related competence can include more than just task-oriented skills. Good employees are often promoted (I was) and this leads to the need for people management skills.

For example, I have seen many excellent accountants promoted to the positions of Controller or Chief Financial Officer. Having spent most of their adult lives studying accounting, many had never studied how to manage people. Those who took the time to learn management skills did well. Others who did not struggled. I even heard of one CFO who was besieged with personnel issues and was overheard saying the answer to his problems could not be found in a book.

Managing people requires a new set of work-related skills that are quite different from task-oriented skills.

Gradual Improvement

As is the case with all the other actions I have discussed so far, learning to be competent in both social and job-related activities took me a lot of time, self-control, study, practice, and mistakes. But competence has never been all or nothing. There are always varying levels.

I started out in life without any manners, and I often offended people. Then I learned a few manners and offended people less often. Eventually, I got better and seldom offended anyone.

I started every job in my life feeling lost and incompetent. Then I would learn to do a few simple things, like how to use the intercom or order supplies, and I would feel a little better. Then I would learn how to do a few more difficult things, like handle a customer call or prepare a report, and I would feel even better. Only after I had learned and practiced many different job-related activities would I start to feel comfortable about what I was doing. It always took time. It always took self-control. It always took learning how to do new things. It always took lots of practice. And the process always involved me making lots of mistakes.

I have been working on my competence for decades, and I am still far from being completely competent at any of the actions I have been discussing. However, I am way better now than I used to be, and my relationships are far healthier.

As you work to improve your competence, do not expect perfection from yourself, or others. Remember, you do not have to be perfect to build healthy relationships. And the people you attempt to build healthy relationships with will not be perfect either.

As you improve your competence, though, your relationships will get better.

Summary

Competence is the quality of my skills in both social and work-related activities. I must improve both before people will trust me more than they do now.

Social activities include manners and communication. Manners are socially acceptable behaviors that can help prevent me from offending others. Competent communication requires empathetic listening and empathetic talking.

Work-related competence can include both task-oriented skills as well as people management skills.

*   *   *

Before reading the next chapter, you might want to try this Competence Exercise:

Competence Exercise

1. Think about someone who does not trust you as much as you wish they would.
2. Can you recall a time you offended them with bad manners?
3. Can you recall a time you upset them because your communication lacked empathy?
4. How could you have handled those situations better?
5. To repair the relationship, try to empathetically explain you are trying to become a better version of yourself, and you realize you may have upset them earlier.
6. Politely apologize for how you acted.
7. Ask them how they felt about how you acted.
8. Empathetically listen to them.
9. Politely apologize again if needed.
10. Going forward, be mindful to use good manners and empathetic communication with them whenever you interact.
11. Observe how your relationship changes as you act more competently towards them.

Study Group Questions

1. Why is it essential to get someone's attention before saying anything important to them?

2. How can we help each other during these meetings to improve our empathetic communication skills?
3. Why is trust situational?
4. Would anyone like to share your experience starting a new job and how your level of competence changed over time?
5. Would anyone like to share your experience being promoted into a management position without having been trained how to manage people?
6. Would anyone like to share your experience with the Competence Exercise?

Chapter 11

Who is Worthy of My Trust?

Once I clearly understood what I had to do if I hoped to increase my chances of having other people trust me, I was then able to use this knowledge to evaluate other people to determine if they were worthy of my trust.

I noticed I had what I referred to as a *trust meter*. It seemed to automatically generate a gut feeling of trust, or distrust, toward each person I met. With some people I met, I felt like I trusted them immediately, as if I had known them all my life. With other people I met, though, I immediately felt like I did not trust them, nor would I ever trust them.

I decided this trust meter had to be a gift from my DNA-soup and historic baggage.

Some of the gut feelings I experienced had to be the result of generations of genetic mutations that must have aided my ancestors in survival and procreation. My DNA-soup could supply my trust meter with any of the following feelings:

> *Trust family, or anyone who looks like them.*
> *Trust tribe members, or anyone who fits in.*
> *Trust (and mate with) anyone beautiful.*
> *Don't trust anyone who is different.*
> *Don't trust anyone ugly.*
> *Don't trust anything that snarls.*

Other gut feelings must have come straight out of my historic baggage, generating feelings like this:

> *Trust anyone who seems nice.*
> *Trust anyone who looks like a friend.*
> *Trust anyone who wants to help.*
> *Don't trust anyone who might hurt me.*
> *Don't trust anyone who might leave me.*
> *Don't trust anyone who might steal from me.*

Sometimes, my trust meter was correct. Sometimes it was not. It appeared to all depend on chance, and I realized my trust meter was illogical and flawed. It did not accurately predict the trustworthiness of others any more than I could accurately predict the outcome of a coin toss.

For example, if I call *heads* every time I flip a coin, in the long run, I will be right half the time. Does that mean I am good at predicting the outcome of a coin toss? Of course not.

And yet, when my trust meter was right, it reinforced my belief in it. Unfortunately, it seemed to be wrong just as often as it was right. And when it was wrong, it led me to doubt my ability to accurately judge the character of people.

Every con artist I might ever meet will depend on me trusting them so they can take advantage of me. If they present themselves in such a way the needle on my trust meter swings to *trust*, then I will be more likely to drop my defenses which is exactly what they hope I will do.

On the other hand, any prejudice or bigotry I ever felt must have sprung forth from my trust meter immediately swinging towards *distrust*, even though I may have known nothing about the person I had just met.

I decided I should never trust my trust meter or any of the gut feelings it generates. Instead, I need to trust only my logical and reasoned evaluation of the trustworthiness of every person I meet.

That means I must refuse to trust or distrust people when I first meet them. I have to remain skeptical. I also have to stay self-aware to monitor any gut feelings being generated by my trust meter so I can remind myself those gut feelings are not trustworthy. And regardless whether my trust meter is sending out trust or distrust signals, I must judge each person I meet only by the following:

> *Do they act with honesty?*
> *Do they act with integrity?*
> *Do they act with compassion?*
> *Do they act with empathy?*
> *Do they act with competence?*

Finding answers to these questions always takes time. That is why it is important I do not judge quickly. As I interact with someone new and focus my attention on them, they eventually reveal their true selves through their actions. If I stay skeptical and observant, I get answers.

After I had clarified what I should look for when determining if someone is worthy of my trust, I decided to reevaluate the people already in my life. Whether I had been trusting someone or distrusting them, I asked myself these same five questions of each person. Through this process, I came to better understand who was, and who was not, trustworthy. The answers reinforced my trust of some of the people and reinforced my distrust of others.

I also discovered my trust levels in a few people were ill-founded. It was the clarity I gained by answering these questions that led me to realize my previous viewpoints about them had been wrong. I realized I should trust some people I had previously distrusted, and I needed to stop trusting a few people I had previously trusted. So, I changed my relationships with them.

Regardless of my answers to these questions, the increased clarity those answers provided helped me make better relationship decisions and gave me the confidence to act on those decisions.

By surrounding myself with trustworthy people, and keeping untrustworthy people out of my life, I have watched the overall health of all my relationships improve.

Summary

The better I understood the trustworthy action groups, the better I became at spotting them with others. By understanding the trustworthiness of people better, I was then able to improve my relationship decisions, and my confidence to act on those decisions increased.

Surrounding myself with trustworthy people, and keeping untrustworthy people out of my life, has improved the overall health of all my relationships.

* * *

Before reading the next chapter, you might want to try this Who is Worthy of My Trust? Exercise:

Who is Worthy of My Trust? Exercise

1. Think of someone in your life you trust.
2. Do they act with honesty?
3. Do they act with integrity?
4. Do they act with compassion?
5. Do they act with empathy?
6. Do they act with competence?
7. Are they worthy of your trust?
8. List examples of their actions that support your answers.
9. Change your relationship with this person if you decide they are not worthy of the trust you have been giving them.
10. Think of someone in your life you do not trust.
11. Do they act with honesty?
12. Do they act with integrity?
13. Do they act with compassion?
14. Do they act with empathy?
15. Do they act with competence?
16. Are they worthy of your trust?
17. List examples of their actions that support your answers.
18. Change your relationship with this person if you decide they are worthy of more trust than you have been giving them.

Study Group Questions

1. Would anyone like to share a time when you trusted someone immediately, but realized later the person was not worthy of your trust?
2. Would anyone like to share a time when you distrusted someone immediately, but realized later the person was worthy of your trust?
3. Would anyone like to share your experience with the Who is Worthy of My Trust? Exercise?

PART THREE:

HEALTHY RELATIONSHIPS

Chapter 12

Relationship Groups

My life has always been filled with relationships.

My first relationships were established at birth with my parents and our family doctor. They were there to take care of me because, as a newborn, I was not able to care for myself. As I grew older, I developed relationships with my brother and two sisters, aunts, uncles, cousins, and friends. Along the way, I met neighbors, teachers, and classmates. I eventually became self-aware, and slowly developed a relationship with myself, but that was quite a bit later. When I entered the workforce, I was introduced to bosses, co-workers, and eventually employees who reported to me. Corky and I bonded, and she became my spouse. We brought two children into our lives and adopted pets.

All the while, I was surrounded with casual acquaintances and strangers.

I had so many relationships in my life, it was difficult to keep track of them, let alone make time for all of them.

Some of these relationships, like my family and friends, had been more important to me than the others. And yet, I had spent more time with bosses, co-workers, and employees who reported to me than I had with family and friends, even though I valued my family and friends more.

As I thought about all the different relationships in my life, I knew some of them were good relationships, and others were bad. Some people I knew quite well while others not as well. I barely knew some of my acquaintances, like neighbors who I waved to even though I did not know their names. And yet, I still had relationships with them, although they were certainly not close relationships.

I also realized the relationships I had with the people I cared about the most were quite different from the relationships I had with people I barely knew.

Needing a way to figure out which relationships were healthy, and which were not, I eventually decided the best way to think about all these relationships was to organize them into groups based on how much I cared about the people involved. I wanted to limit the number of groups to as few as possible while including every relationship I had.

I came up with these four groups:

- Loved-ones
- Co-workers
- Acquaintances
- Strangers

I decided not to list family or friends as separate groups because I did not have the same level of compassion for all the members of my family or all my friends. Therefore, I did not want them to be lumped together in the same group. Each family member or friend was either a loved-one, a co-worker, an acquaintance, or a stranger. It all depended on how I interacted with them and how much I cared about them.

Looking for a graphic representation of these relationship groups, I settled on concentric circles that surrounded me at the center (see figure 2).

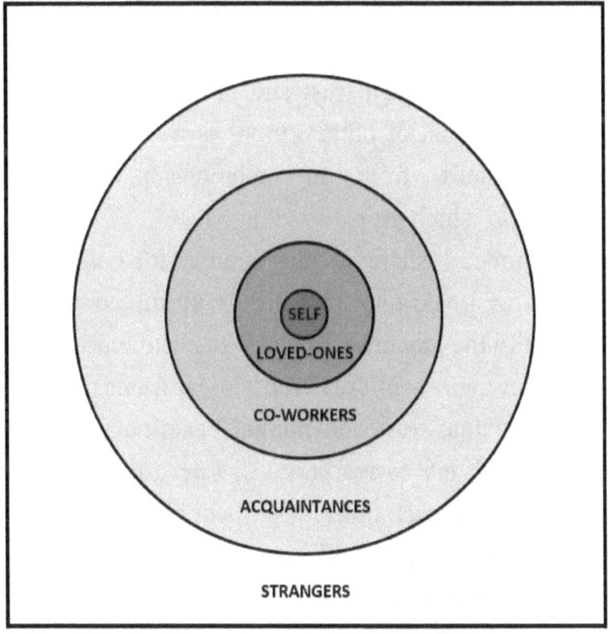

Figure 2 – Relationship Groups

My loved-ones, inside the ring closest to me, are closer to me emotionally than anyone else in my life. They are my most important relationships and the dearest to my heart. My loved-ones include my wife, children, pets, and best friends. Moving out from my loved-ones, each subsequent ring contains those relationships that are the next closest and important to me. My co-workers are more important to me than my acquaintances, but less important than my loved-ones. And my acquaintances are more important to me than strangers, but less important than my co-workers.

Once I had my relationships organized into groups, I was then able to clarify what a healthy relationship looked like inside each group. For a relationship to be healthy, I knew it had to be built on mutual trust and provide mutual benefit. However, the amount of mutual trust, as well as the amount of mutual benefit, from any relationship would vary depending on in which group it belonged.

For example, I share greater mutual trust and mutual benefit with my loved-ones than I do with my co-workers. I cannot quantify the amount of mutual trust and mutual benefit I share with my wife, children, and closest friends. But I can quantify the mutual trust and mutual benefit I share in my relationships with my co-workers. All I need to do is look at how much we trust each other, what benefits I provide them, and what benefits they provide me. Although it is less than what I share with my loved-ones, it is far greater than what I share with any of my acquaintances.

Another thing I realized was the word *mutual*, within the context of my relationships, does not mean *equal*. In other words, I can have a healthy relationship with someone even if they trust me more than I trust them, or they benefit more from our relationship than I do.

Equality is not important. What is important is we both benefit more from our relationship than the time and energy we each invest in it.

For example, whenever I am with a client, my goal is to help them in such a way the benefit they receive is far more valuable to them than the money they pay me. At the same time, I want the money they paid me to be more valuable to me than the time I spend with them. On top of that, they need to trust me to help them, and I need to trust them to pay me. When that all happens, we have mutual trust, mutual benefit, and a healthy relationship. We trust each other and both of us benefit more from our relationship than it costs us.

This is why healthy relationships tend to last a long time. As long as both parties are benefiting from their relationship, neither one will want it to end.

However, if the value of the time and energy needed by one person to maintain a relationship is greater than the benefit they receive from it, then that relationship would have to be unhealthy *for that person* even if the other person was happy with it. A healthy relationships must be healthy for both people, otherwise, the benefits will not be mutual.

A few years after opening my consulting business, I had a client who asked me to discount my hourly rate because he felt I was too expensive for his business to afford. I ended our relationship because if he thought the value he received from my services was less than what my services cost him, then I knew our relationship would not be healthy for him. And if I discounted my hourly rate to make him happy, then our relationship would not be healthy for me. And whenever I have an unhealthy relationship in my life, it is important to me I act immediately to either heal it or end it. In this case, I could not find any way for us both to feel good about the benefits we were receiving from our relationship. Therefore, it was better for us both that I ended it.

In the next chapter, I will discuss the circle at the center of all my relationship groups, me, and what a healthy relationship with myself looks like and why that is important.

In the following chapters, I will discuss each of the other relationship groups and how I evaluate healthy relationships within them. The last chapter is my take on soulmates, what they are and how to find one.

Summary

My life is filled with relationships. Understanding the health of each is easier for me when I group them into four general categories based on how much I care about the people within each group. These groups are:

- Loved-Ones
- Co-Workers
- Acquaintances
- Strangers

For a relationship to be healthy, it must be built on mutual trust and provide mutual benefit. However, *mutual* does not mean *equal*.

A healthy relationship exists when both parties trust each other, and they receive benefits from each other which are greater than the time and energy they each devote to that relationship.

* * *

Before reading the next chapter, you might want to try this Relationship Groups Exercise:

Relationship Groups Exercise

1. Draw four columns on a blank sheet of paper
2. At the top of the columns, write the names of the relationship groups, one for each column.
3. Think about the relationships you have with your friends. Who would you consider to be a loved-one?
4. List their names in the column underneath where you wrote *Loved-ones*.
5. How would you classify the rest of your friends?
6. List their names in the columns underneath where you wrote *Co-workers*, *Acquaintances*, or *Strangers*.
7. Look at the paper and think about how different your relationships are with the friends you listed in different columns.
8. Draw the same four columns on another sheet of blank paper and label them the same way.
9. Think about the relationships you have with your family members, both immediate family and extended family.
10. Who would you consider to be a loved-one?
11. List their names in the column underneath where you wrote *Loved-ones*.
12. How would you classify the rest of your family members?

13. List their names in the columns underneath where
    you wrote *Co-workers*, *Acquaintances*, or *Strangers*.
14. Look at the paper and think about how different your
    relationships are with the family members you listed
    in different columns.

Study Group Questions

1. What do you think about relationship groups?
2. How do you feel about splitting your friends and
   family into different groups?
3. How can relationship groups help us to better
   understand the different relationships in our lives?
4. How does the level of mutual trust and mutual benefit
   compare between different groups?
5. Would anyone like to share your experience with the
   Relationship Groups Exercise?

Chapter 13

Self

As I attempted to build mutual trust with the people in my life as I described in *Part Two*, I discovered I could not make much progress with others until I improved the relationship I had with myself. That is why I labeled the center circle of the *Relationship Groups* as *Self*. It represents the relationship I have with myself.

The first thing I had to do was accept the idea I had a relationship with myself. It is the life I live inside my head, how I view myself, and how I view the world around me. Although it sounds a bit self-centered, the relationship I had with myself turned out to be the most important relationship in my life because the healthier the relationship I had with myself, the better I became at relating to others.

I found the best way to test the health of the relationship I have with myself is to engage my self-awareness and ask myself this one simple question:

Do I trust myself?

Relationships are complicated. Life is complicated. If I do not trust myself to build healthy relationships or run my own life, then I need to fix whatever is wrong with me so I can become worthy of my own trust. After all, I certainly do not want anyone else running my life or telling me what to do. So, I need to trust myself to do it.

Whenever I ask myself this question (and I ask it often), I observe how I respond to it, both emotionally and intellectually. If I feel comfortable emotionally and the intellectual answer is *yes*, then I think I have a relatively healthy relationship with myself. On the other hand, if I feel negative emotions like anger or sadness (like after I do something especially stupid like getting fired for fighting with my partner) and the intellectual answer is *no*, then I know the health of my relationship with myself needs improvement.

Most of the time, my response to this question falls somewhere between these two extremes of healthy and unhealthy. I might trust myself in some areas, like taking care of our finances (because we have made good money and managed it well), but not in other areas such as taking care of my health (because I continue to struggle with my weight and do not always eat properly or exercise as I should).

And of course, my relationship with myself is not like the relationships I have with others. If I do not trust someone, I can avoid them. But I cannot avoid myself. I have tried. It does not work. No matter where I go, there I am, sitting three inches behind my eyeballs looking out on the world around me (at least it feels that way).

I could just ignore myself, but I would do that at my own peril for one of the long-term consequences of not trusting myself is that building and maintaining healthy relationships with others is nearly impossible. How can I expect someone to trust me if I do not trust myself? Therefore, my top priority is always to be worthy of my own trust.

Whenever I feel like I am not worthy of my own trust, I know I must not be doing one, or more, of the trustworthy action groups with myself. I might be doing any or all the following:

- not being honest with myself
- not keeping promises to myself
- not being compassionate with myself
- not being empathetic with myself
- lacking the competence I need to interact with myself and live my life

Honesty with Self

Do I confront the truth about myself, or do I mislead myself into thinking things are different than they are?

For example, I started smoking when I was sixteen because I wanted to be cool and have the cool kids like me. I never believed the claims that it was bad for me, and even after I developed an ongoing smoker's cough, frequent colds, and sinus problems, I still refused to admit it had anything to do with cigarettes. I typically blamed it on my allergies. Besides, I only smoked half a pack a day, that was not as much as a lot of smokers I knew.

The truth was I was being dishonest with myself. And I did it for eleven years. Whenever I would start to think about my smoking, I would change the subject in my mind and think about something else. I got quite good at it too. There was a lot going on in my life, so switching my attention was not difficult.

This is the first lesson I learned from my smoking:

If I am avoiding thinking about my behavior,
I am probably doing something I shouldn't.

Of course, I did not learn this lesson at that time. This realization came to me much later.

When I was twenty-seven and Corky was pregnant with our daughter, I took a hard look at my health and realized smoking was bad for me (and just plain stupid). So, I quit. And every day after that, I yearned for a cigarette (thank you, historic baggage).

During an after-work happy hour five years later, I was feeling a little tipsy from a couple of drinks and decided to show off. I lit a cigarette for a co-worker, inhaled, and blew a smoke ring.

Big mistake.

The cravings intensified. I kept the cigarette and smoked it myself, and that started me smoking again.

This time, however, I smoked much less than before, maybe two or three cigarettes a day. And I did not tell my family about it. I only smoked where they would not catch me, and I devised a simple way to hide the smell. Before going home, I would peel an orange and eat it. The citrus smell would get all over my hands and inside my mouth, concealing all evidence of my unhealthy behavior.

I smoked in secret for five years. During that time, I shifted back to my earlier habit of ignoring my behavior and not examining why I was doing it.

Here is another lesson I learned from my smoking which I figured out later:

If I am hiding my actions from my family,
I am probably doing something I shouldn't.

When I was thirty-seven, I decided we should probably get some life insurance. When I looked into it, I found out life insurance companies did not agree with me that having a couple of cigarettes a day was no big deal. If I had smoked even one cigarette within the last twelve months, then I was a tobacco user and the premium would be almost double.

That got me thinking.

If having one cigarette a year would double my life insurance premium, then smoking a couple a day must be even worse for my health (actuarially speaking).

I decided it was time to get completely honest with myself. Why was I smoking?

I came up with many reasons. It calmed me down when I was stressed. It allowed me some quiet time to think (about everything but smoking). It suppressed my appetite. It made me feel competent because I did it well (I could French inhale and blow smoke rings). And because smoking was considered a bad habit, it made me feel like a rebel who did not let anyone tell him what he could or could not do.

Then it struck me.

I smoked because I still wanted to be cool. I wanted to fit in with the cool kids, and I wanted to be liked. My initial desire and decision to start smoking twenty-one years earlier was still with me, even though it made absolutely no sense.

Talk about historic baggage!

Here is the most important lesson from my smoking habit that I figured out later:

The true source of my repeated bad behavior
is usually my original reasoning that started
me acting that way in the first place.

So, I quit again. This time, the cravings were far less. I still felt them, but when I did, I would think about how trying to be cool by smoking made no sense. I would also visualize coughing, phlegm accumulation, and sinus problems.

Fourteen years later, I was on vacation in London and having a pint in the Goat Pub with a friend of mine (I used to smoke with him back when I was smoking in secret). My friend was smoking, and I was feeling a little tipsy (again). When the craving for a cigarette hit me, I lit one without thinking and smoked it.

When I finished, I realized I did not enjoy it. That was interesting. The last time I had not enjoyed a cigarette was when I was first learning how to smoke.

So, I smoked another one to see what would happen. I did not enjoy that one either, and I realized I no longer felt any desire to smoke.

That was in 2004, and I have not had a cigarette since. In addition, I have felt no craving for one (even when tipsy). I have occasionally felt something weaker than a craving, like a faint shadow of a craving, but it has been easy to ignore.

It took complete honesty with myself to quit smoking for good. The flip side of that statement is it took continuous dishonesty with myself to continue smoking. If I want to trust myself, being honest about my bad behavior is crucial.

However, it is also important I am honest about my good behavior and accomplishments. When I feel sad or depressed, it is easy to focus on my shortcomings and then belittle myself for them. I have made a lot of mistakes in my life and beating myself up about them is easy to do. How can I possibly trust myself when I am such a screw up?

But this generalized attitude does not ring true. When I am honest with myself, I must admit I have made far more good decisions in my life than bad ones. So, this feeling must be coming from my historic baggage. Belittling myself is just another form of dishonesty.

To trust myself, I must be honest with myself about both the good things in my life and the bad things.

Another area that requires total honesty with myself is how I view my body. In tenth grade, my best friend, Doug, had six-pack abs, something I had always wanted but never achieved. When we played basketball together, Doug never wore a shirt. At home afterwards, I would look at myself in the mirror and cringe. I looked horrible in comparison. Long after high school, I continued to consider myself to be a big, fat slob because I did not have Doug's six-pack abs.

This was another form of dishonesty. Just because I did not look like Doug, did not mean I was a big, fat slob.

What helped me to take a more honest view of my body was reading an anatomy book. I was amazed to learn the average human body contains over 32 trillion cells (over four thousand times the total human population of earth). Each cell relies on the others to live, but they all have a life of their own. And of course, I depend on my cells to work together and function as a body for *me* to inhabit.

Not to get too philosophical here, but the *me* I am referring to in that last sentence is my self-aware, thinking consciousness. The *me* Descartes referred to as thinking, and therefore existing. The *me* that feels like I am looking out on the world from behind these two eyeballs.

Once I stopped thinking of my body as *me* or even *my body*, I was able to start thinking of it as something that is separate and distinct from me. It is my community of cells. This change in my viewpoint allowed me to focus more on keeping my community of cells healthy and less on criticizing myself for not having Doug's six-pack abs.

Integrity with Self

Do I keep the promises I make to myself, or do I promise to do things and then not do them, or promise to not do things and then do them anyway?

Just as it is important in my relationships with others that I do not make promises I might not be able to keep, it is just as important to not make promises to myself I might not be able to keep. If I regularly break promises to myself, how can I trust myself to keep my promises in the future?

For example, making another New Year's resolution to lose twenty pounds by March is pointless if I have failed to keep that same promise to myself for the previous five years in a row (yes, I really did that).

I eventually found a better promise I could make to myself I knew I could keep. I promised I would research weight loss and find something that might actually work for me long-term (yes, I did this too, and it did work for me).

If I am going to trust myself, I need to know I am going to do what I say I am going to do. For me, that starts with only making promises to myself I know I can keep. If I am not absolutely positive I can keep my promise, then I only promise myself I will try.

I know, this sounds a bit lame, but it is better than making and then breaking a promise to myself.

Compassion for Self

It seemed to me that caring about myself should be easy. Afterall, I certainly have a vested interest in my welfare. But over time, I realized consistently caring about myself was not easy at all. So, I came up with a couple questions I could ask myself to see how I felt about myself.

Do I care enough about myself to ask myself how I am doing, and then be honest enough to tell myself the truth?

After we lost our son, Richard, in 2008, I had to constantly remind myself I was grieving and cut myself some slack. I was not doing well at all, and I had to accept that fact and not pretend everything was fine. I also had to care enough about myself to allow myself to feel sad and even cry if I felt the need. It was the hardest thing I ever did, but if I had not treated myself with kindness and caring during that time, I could easily have spiraled into a pit of despair I may never have climbed my way out of.

Do I care enough about myself to forgive myself for my past mistakes?

As you are probably well aware by now, I have made many, many, many, many mistakes in my life. Regardless how much I may want to change the past, it will always remain completely beyond my control. There is no way I can undo what I have done.

What I can do, however, is learn from my mistakes. Then, I can take that knowledge and change my current behavior and work to improve my future.

Even Hollywood recognizes I can never undo what I have done, but I can always do the right thing next.

Yes, you made a mistake, but it is what you do next that matters the most.

Tom Selleck
as Frank Reagan
in Blue Bloods

Sometimes, after I do something stupid, like reacting to something Corky says and we end up in an argument, I do not like myself very much. When this happens, I sometimes let my emotions take over, and I suspend my self-awareness, long-term perspective, and self-control. When that happens, I can start to feel like a screw-up and stop caring about myself.

Once I stop caring about myself, I often stop taking care of myself. I might stay up too late, or drink too much, or eat too much. There have been times when I have done all three. This unhealthy behavior can then start a downward spiral toward self-loathing. In addition to not liking myself for arguing with Corky, I also feel the effects of my actions against myself. I might be tired from too little sleep, or hung over from too much alcohol, or bloated from too much food, making me feel even worse about myself.

The only successful path I have found to pull myself out of this downward spiral has been to force myself to exercise my self-awareness again. I must make myself look at what I am doing and ask myself, "Does this make sense?"

Once I realize I am under the influence (once again) of my DNA-soup or historic baggage, then I can refocus on my long-term perspective and start to exert my self-control. This then allows me to take responsible action to deal with my mistake and forgive myself.

Is it easy? No. Do I struggle to do this? Yes.

Will I ever be perfect at it? No, but I also know perfection is an unrealistic expectation.

As I have practiced caring for myself, I have gotten better at taking care of myself and my life. And the better I have gotten at taking care of myself and my life, the better I have felt about myself which then has encouraged me to better care for myself. I can attest this upward spiral of self-esteem feels far better than the downward spiral of self-loathing. I just have to remember to care about myself enough to forgive my past mistakes and work diligently to become the best version of myself as I move forward in my life.

Empathy with Self

To have empathy for someone means I try to see the world as they see it. If I applied that definition to myself, I would try to see the world as I see it, which I always do. I look at the world, and I see it as I see it. That does not mean I see it accurately; it just means I see it from my viewpoint.

Since that definition does not help me with my relationship with myself, I decided to define being empathetic with myself as *questioning* my viewpoint. In other words, if I am not being empathetic with myself, then I have stopped questioning my viewpoint and started assuming it is accurate just because it is mine (which never helps my relationships).

Since I can be influenced by my DNA-soup and historic baggage, it is not enough to see the world as I see it. I must exert enough energy to be self-aware and ask myself if my interpretation of the world makes sense, because if I ever hope to change my opinion about something or someone, I have to first realize my current opinion may be wrong.

For example, when I first met Corky, I did not like her. I thought she was arrogant and mean. As I interacted with her over the months following our initial meeting, however, I found evidence to the contrary. She was humble and kind. I had to reevaluate my opinion of her based on these new experiences. I eventually realized my first impression of her was wrong, probably influenced by my historic baggage. Had

I held on to my original opinion, Corky and I would never have created a life together.

Journaling was the one thing I found that helped me better understand my worldview and evaluate if it made sense. I first started journaling while at tech school in Mississippi after I had read *The Fountainhead* by Ayn Rand. I was spending a lot of time alone in the barracks studying the books I found in the branch library, and I needed some way to sort through all the thoughts swirling in my head.

At that time, I did not feel I had anyone with whom I could discuss what I was learning. The guys in the barracks certainly did not seem interested. So, I bought a spiral notebook and wrote my first entry on November 5th, 1972.

> 5 NOV 72
>
> IF YOU RELIVE YOUR DAY AND FIND ACTIONS WHICH CONFLICT WITH YOUR OWN IDEAS OF WHAT YOU ARE, YOUR LIEING TO YOUR SELF.
>
> NOT UNTIL A PERSON CAN BE COMPLETELY HONEST WITH HIMSELF CAN HE ATTAIN TRUE HAPPINESS.

It says:

> *If you relive your day and find actions which*
> *conflict with your own ideas of what you are,*
> *your lieing* (sic) *to yourself.*

> *Not until a person can be completely honest*
> *with himself can he attain true happiness.*

I never was very good at grammar or spelling, and I never bothered to proof what I wrote in my journal. Still, not too bad for a first journal entry, especially considering I was only nineteen. And it was certainly a philosophical improvement over my, *"The future is nothing more than a dream,"* quote I had submitted to the yearbook committee three years earlier during my senior year in high school.

I liked to journal my assumptions and opinions as if they belonged to someone who was speaking to me. I found this helped me to separate myself from the entries I was making. That separation then allowed me to analyze whether they made sense to me, and it enabled me to let go of any assumptions or opinions I may have had that conflicted with my new thoughts and experiences.

The more I studied, the more I journaled. It helped me to sort through what I was learning and organize it with what I felt like I already understood.

Since my worldview belonged to me, I figured I might as well take control of it and mold it into a worldview that made sense to me and was aligned with my newly forming long-term perspective.

Competence with Self

Being competent at running my life is critical if I want to trust myself. Even if I treat myself with honesty, integrity, compassion, and empathy, I will not trust myself if I am not competent at taking care of myself or my life.

Whenever I have ignored my body and ate whatever I wanted and did not exercise, I stopped trusting myself. My weight would balloon, my lower back would hurt, and I would not like how I looked or felt.

After I read the anatomy book and began viewing my body as my community of cells, I started taking better care of myself for I realized I depended on my community of cells to live. At the same time, my community of cells depended on me to make healthy choices so each cell could have the nutrition it needed to survive and cooperate with the other cells to keep the community functioning as a whole.

It felt a little like owning a dog. I would take care of my dog because I wanted her to be healthy and have a good life. And I wanted to take care of my community of cells (body) for the same reason. I wanted each member to be healthy and have a good life.

*   *   *

A brief personal aside: As I sit here reworking this section of the book on May 7, 2020, the Novel Coronavirus is spreading around the world with dire consequences.

I have been working on this book for over two years now, and there are times when I wonder if I will ever finish it.

I got quite sick two months ago, and I wondered if I had COVID-19. At 67, I am high risk for mortality. Was I going to die before I published this book? Man, that would suck!

I still do not know if I had the coronavirus, COVID-19, or something else. There was no testing available in San Diego for anyone who was not in respiratory distress, which I was not. I probably just had the flu or a nasty cold. I do not know. What I do know, however, is my community of cells pulled together and fought off whatever it was. Well done!

Part of everyone's community of cells is an army of cells that have evolved to attack anything that is harmful to the rest of the community. Like any army, these cells require proper nutrition and exercise so they are prepared to do their job.

I guess I have been providing my cells with the nutrition and exercise they need because my army fought off whatever it was that had invaded my community of cells. Had I not been taking care of myself these past few decades, this book may never have been finished, let alone published.

Just thought you might like the update.

Now, I will get back to it…

*   *   *

To trust myself, I must pay attention to, be responsible for, and be competent at many things.

Whenever I have ignored my self-awareness and allowed my DNA-soup and historic baggage to influence my actions, I stopped trusting myself for I would walk around in a foul mood, fight with my loved-ones, and hate my life. If I ignored my finances and spent more money than I made, I stopped trusting myself for I would go deeper into debt, buy things I did not need, and wonder if I would ever be able to dig my way out. If I ignored my mind and stopped learning new things, I stopped trusting myself for I would begin to feel like my life had stagnated. If I was no longer growing as a person, what was I doing here?

To trust myself, I must be competent at handling my life. The good news is, I do not have to know how to do everything. Thankfully, there are trustworthy people out there who can help me, I just need to find them and build healthy relationships with them.

For example, I do not need to know how to fix my car. I do need to make sure my car receives the service it needs to keep running, but I do not need to learn how to do it myself. And since I do not want to learn how to do it, I found someone I trust to do it for me.

There are many things in my life I am not good at doing. I am not good at plumbing, remodeling my house, repairing appliances, drafting legal documents, and many other things. But my job is to run my life. That does not mean I have to do everything myself; it just means I have to be responsible enough to ensure everything is done and done correctly.

And whenever I have done that, I have trusted myself because I was worthy of my own trust. And that became my definition of having a healthy relationship with myself.

Summary

The most important relationship in my life is the one I have with myself.

Without a healthy relationship with myself, I will struggle to establish healthy relationships with others, even if I improve both my trustworthy action groups and my ability to spot them in others.

A good test of my relationship with myself is to engage my self-awareness and ask myself this question:

Do I trust myself?

If my answer to this question is *no*, I must not be doing one, or more, of the trustworthy action groups with myself. I might be doing any or all the following:

- not being honest with myself
- not keeping promises to myself
- not being compassionate with myself
- not being empathetic with myself
- lacking the competence I need to interact with myself and live my life

If I do not trust myself, then I need to fix whatever is wrong with me so I can become worthy of my own trust.

* * *

Before reading the next chapter, you might want to try these Self Exercises:

Self Exercises

Start a personal journal.

1. Engage your self-awareness and think about how you feel about writing in a journal.
2. Promise yourself you will write something in a journal every day for the next seven days.
3. Observe how you feel about making this promise. Are you happy about starting a journal? Are you afraid you may not keep your promise to yourself?

4. Find something you want to use as your journal. You could use a leather-bound, store-bought journal with hundreds of blank pages just waiting for you to fill them in with all your thoughts and ideas, or you could use a plain legal pad, or a spiral binder, or a Word document on your computer, or an Excel spreadsheet, or the notepad on your phone. It does not matter. Whatever makes you comfortable. Afterall, it is your journal.

5. Write your first entry into your journal. Write the date. Write how you feel about writing in this journal. Write whatever else you feel like writing.

6. Tomorrow, write something new in your journal.

7. After seven days, write how you feel about writing in your journal and compare it to your first entry.

Improve the health of your relationship with yourself.

1. Engage your self-awareness and ask yourself this question, "Do I trust myself?"

2. Observe your emotional reaction. Write how you feel in your journal.

3. Observe your intellectual reaction. Write what you think in your journal.

4. List what you could improve about yourself that would help you trust yourself more.

5. Pick one thing on your list and practice improving it for the next 24 hours.

6. After 24 hours, write in your journal about your experience improving one thing.
7. Repeat steps 1-7 until you trust yourself more.

Study Group Questions

1. Why is your relationship with yourself so important?
2. Would anyone like to share a time you struggled to be honest with yourself?
3. Would anyone like to share a time you broke a promise to yourself?
4. Has anyone ever felt like you did not care about yourself?
5. What can we do to become more competent at running our lives?
6. Would anyone like to share your experience with the Self Exercises?

Chapter 14

Loved-Ones

When I think about what a healthy relationship with a loved-one should look like, it always includes the highest level of mutual trust and mutual benefit.

For example, Corky and I have built a life together from which we have both benefited greatly. And I cannot imagine trusting anyone more than I trust her. We brought two children into this world and have loved them deeply. And all four of us have benefited from the family we created together.

The same holds true for my closest friends whom I love. Although I have not spent as much time with them as I would like, the mutual trust and mutual benefit we have shared has been significant.

To be clear, a loved-one is not necessarily someone I have fallen in love with. *Falling in love* is something that happens to me. I have no control over it. Love, the feeling, is an emotion, and I cannot control my emotions. Emotional love may or may not be coming from my DNA-soup or historic baggage. It may or may not make sense. It may or may not be good for me because a person I fall in love with may or may not be worthy of my trust.

It saddens me whenever I read about someone whose life was ruined by falling in love with someone who was not trust-worthy. Untrustworthy people are not worthy of my love because they are not worthy of my trust. Regardless how strong I may feel love for them, any attempt to build a relationship with someone who is not worthy of my trust is doomed to failure.

As weird as this sounds, in matters of the heart, it has been better for me to rely on my logic and reason than it has been to listen to my heart. Logic and reason may not have filled my tummy with butterflies, but logic and reason have certainly helped me avoid chasing a butterfly off a cliff.

A true loved-one is someone I choose to love. *To love*, the verb. It is something I do, not something I feel. I may also feel love for them, of course, but that is not something I can control. I have found, though, the feeling of love for someone typically does follow the action of loving them.

To love someone means I treat them with honesty, integrity, compassion, empathy, and competence as described in Part Two. And I do it all the time. At least I try to do it all the time (I am not perfect).

Loving someone means I put their needs ahead of my own, and that requires a commitment of my time. To love someone properly, I must devote enough time to them to build a strong bond of mutual trust. If I tried to love too many people, I would not have enough time to love each one of them fully. I might feel love for a thousand people, but I cannot imagine how one lifetime would be long enough to build healthy relationships with a thousand loved-ones.

The relationship group I call *Loved-ones* can include spouses, children, extended family members, friends, or even pets. I may not have control over the love I feel for them, but I do have control over the time I spend showing them how much I love them.

They deserve my trust, my time, and my love.

Summary

A healthy relationship with a loved-one is evidenced by a heightened level of mutual trust and mutual benefit. A loved-one is someone I have chosen to love, and to love someone means I treat them with honesty, integrity, compassion, empathy, and competence all the time.

* * *

Before reading the next chapter, you might want to try this Loved-Ones Exercise:

Loved-Ones Exercise

1. Engage your self-awareness and ask yourself this question, "Who in my life deserves my love the most?"
2. Write down how you feel and what you think about this question.
3. Write down your answer to the question.
4. Write down why this person deserves your love more than anyone else.
5. Write down a list of things you can do you think this person would appreciate.
6. Pick one item on the list and do it tomorrow.

7. Write down what happened when you did it. How did you feel? How did they respond? Was it a good choice?
8. Update your list based on your new understanding.
9. Pick another item and do it the next day.
10. Write down what happened when you did it. How did you feel? How did they respond? Was it a good choice?
11. Update your list based on your new understanding.
12. Repeat steps 9-12 for the rest of your life.

Study Group Questions

1. What is the difference between *love*, the feeling, and *love*, the verb?
2. Would anyone like to share your experience of falling in love with an untrustworthy person?
3. How can we use logic and reason to make better choices in *matters of the heart*?
4. Can we really just choose to love someone because we have determined they are worthy of our trust and love?
5. How can we best show someone we love them?
6. Would anyone like to share your experience with the Loved-Ones Exercise?

Chapter 15

Co-Workers

My relationship group of co-workers includes everyone with whom I have ever worked. It includes peers, bosses, employees who reported to me, and other people who were associated with the companies where I worked, like customers and vendors with whom I interacted.

The healthiest of these relationships were filled with mutual trust and tremendous mutual benefit. Of course, the amount of trust and benefit I received from my co-workers was never as much as I received from my loved-ones, despite having spent far more time with my co-workers.

During my career, I have held many different jobs. Some jobs I loved, and some jobs I hated. Some jobs I did well, and some jobs I did poorly. Most of them were somewhere in between these extremes. I have buffed floors, cleaned toilets, repaired computers, and run a coffee shop. I have painted houses, insulated attics, laid tile, and repaired plumbing. I have sold things at flea markets, door-to-door, along the side of the road, on the phone, and in an office. I have ushered for the San Diego Padres and taken tickets for the Chargers. I have been a janitor, a collector, a loan officer, an office manager, a cultist, a mortgage broker, an accountant, a COO, a CFO, and a business consultant.

Throughout it all, I successfully built healthy relationships with many of my co-workers. I also failed miserably to build healthy relationships with many others.

This is what I learned along the way.

Peers

I found it most helpful to view my peers at work as my teammates. If we worked together, we could help the company achieve its purpose.

As an employee, I always did better when I set aside my personal goals. Whenever I had tried to do what was right for me, as opposed to what was right for the company, it led me into a competitive mindset in which I thought of my peers as opponents. Thinking of my co-workers as opponents created an unhealthy relationship with them because I would never treat an opponent with honesty, integrity, compassion, or empathy since they might use it against me. And the only thing I ever want to do competently with an opponent is to beat them so I can win the competition.

This was the mistake I had made with my partners in the real estate research and consulting business I discussed earlier. I treated them like opponents rather than teammates, and I competed against them to protect my personal interests.

At other companies, though, I viewed my peers as teammates which created a mindset of cooperation rather than competition. That mindset allowed me to treat them with honesty, integrity, compassion, empathy, and competence as we all worked together to help the company succeed.

When I built healthy relationships with my peers based on mutual trust, we often became a highly productive and synergistic team. A synergistic team is one where the ability of the team is greater than the sum of the abilities of its individual members.

For example, when this happens in sports, teams with less talented players can beat teams whose players have greater ability but less mutual trust. Like when the American hockey team in the 1980 Olympics won the gold medal over the heavily favored Soviet Union team which had players with greater individual abilities.

When this happens in business, smaller companies have been able to disrupt entire industries by cooperating and collaborating to solve problems better than their larger competitors with greater resources. Like when Apple Computer's two founders, Steve Jobs and Steve Wozniak, set the computer industry on its head between 1976 and 1980.

In some companies where I have worked, of course, not all my peers have been worthy of my trust. Some were combative, others were not good at their jobs, and others were just annoying. But I had no control over them. I could not make them change. The best I could do was to build healthy relationships with those who were worthy of my trust and hope the others would respond positively to our example. If they did not, then I would do my best to continue to demonstrate my trustworthiness but keep my distance from them and try to avoid conflict by focusing on my work.

Unfortunately, I did not always exercise enough self-control to avoid conflicts. And my family and I suffered the emotional and financial consequences because of it. When my working environment was becoming unbearable, I should have discussed it with my boss or human resources. They had the authority to fix it. If they did not fix it, then I should have just started looking for a job someplace else.

Bosses

Most of the bosses I have worked for in my career have not been very competent at managing people. I believe that is because there are not enough competent managers in the world to fill the need for competent managers. So, many companies promote their best employees into management positions, which I think is a good strategy. Unfortunately, many of these companies often forget to train their new managers on how to manage people effectively.

When I have been lucky enough to work for a good boss, building a healthy relationship was easy. All I did was demonstrate my trustworthiness. A good boss can spot a trustworthy employee and will work well with them.

Since I have not worked for many good bosses, I had to figure out how to build the best relationship I could with bosses who were not worthy of my trust. I started with being worthy of their trust by providing honest feedback whenever they asked for it and doing what I said I was going to do. I also cared about the work we were doing, and I empathized with my bosses by striving to see things as they saw them.

What problems were they trying to solve? How might I help them? Was there a competency they needed I could provide or develop? And I would try to consistently make a productive difference in our area. All of which I figured would have a positive effect on my relationship with them.

It did not always work out that way.

For example, in 1983, my boss at the mortgage servicing company where I worked gave me my first annual review. During my first year in the collections department, I had retrained my peers to improve our efficiency and productivity. I had been advanced from the one-month desk, to the two-month desk, and then to the pre-foreclosure desk faster than anyone in the company's history. I was excited about the review and was hoping to be rewarded with a big raise.

Instead, my boss told me I should look for work someplace else.

I was devastated. After everything I had done over the last year to improve the morale and productivity of his department? I could not believe what I was hearing. When I thought about it later, however, I realized he was probably worried about me taking over his job. So, it did kind of make sense.

That was not the first or last time a boss disappointed me.

Whenever my efforts have not resulted in a healthy relationship with my boss, I would sit back and assess if my boss were someone I should continue helping. If I decided they were a good person, even if not a particularly good manager, then I would keep at it. However, if I decided they were not worthy of my continued support, then I would start looking for a boss someplace else who I would prefer to help.

At the mortgage servicing company, I heard the manager of the commercial loan servicing department was looking for help. When I approached him, he was happy to transfer me into his department. I felt fortunate I did not have to leave the company, and my new boss turned out to be a far more competent manager than my old boss.

Employees

When I have successfully built healthy relationships with my peers and bosses, I was frequently promoted into a management position.

After five years at the mortgage servicing company, I had been promoted out of commercial loan servicing to Corporate Accounting and then to Vice President and Controller.

Whenever I was promoted into a management position, I knew my priorities had to change. My job was no longer doing task-oriented work. It had become supporting the productivity of my staff. So, building healthy relationships with them was crucial.

In my experience, the best employees I ever had always wanted two things from me as their boss. They wanted me to support them, and they wanted me to protect them.

Supporting my employees was primarily getting any barriers out of their way so they could get their jobs done. In other words, get them the tools and supplies they needed to be productive.

For example, if someone's computer was not working, I would get it fixed right away. If a printer was low on ink, I would get a replacement cartridge before the old one ran out.

When it came to protecting my employees, I needed to protect them from being attacked by anyone outside or inside the company. I do not believe *the customer is always right*, and I have defended my staff from belligerent customers (sometimes, without as much empathy for the customer as I probably should have shown). Also, not everyone inside the companies where I worked treated my staff as I wanted them to be treated. So, I have defended them against attacks from other departments and managers (however, I would not recommend charging into another manager's office and yelling at them).

I also needed to defend my employees against any attacks coming from other staff members inside my department.

In his book *Good to Great*, Jim Collins talks about the importance of getting the right people on the team as well as getting the wrong people off the team because one bad employee can destroy a department.

I came to define a bad employee as anyone who was not trustworthy. A dishonest employee may lie to, or steal from, me, the company, a customer, a vendor, or another employee. They can destroy the mutual trust throughout a company. An employee who lacks integrity does not get done what they say they will get done. They can destroy the plans and workflow of a department. An employee who lacks compassion does not care about their job, their peers, or the company. They tend to be the least productive members of the team and will expect everyone else to cover for them, thereby putting an added burden on the rest of the staff. An employee who lacks empathy may not be able to cooperate with the other employees. They can create conflicts and prevent the rest of the team from getting their work done. And an employee who lacks social or job-related skills will not be able to collaborate or cooperate with their peers well enough to contribute to the productivity of the team.

Bad employees bring down everyone's morale.

And I never met an untrustworthy employee who was happy in their job. Since they are unable to produce, they tend to be miserable, constantly waiting to be found out and fired. And they tend to make their manager (me) miserable as well. They do not solve problems. They are a problem that needs to be solved.

One of my top priorities as a manager was to ensure I had the right team members. I needed to identify who was trustworthy, and who was not. This was when I came up with the *magic wand* idea I discussed in chapter eight.

If I suspected someone was not trustworthy, I would ask myself why I thought that. I had to be specific. Maybe I could help them fix the problem.

For example, if they lacked social or work-related skills, perhaps I could get them some training that would help.

On the other hand, if I could not help them fix the problem, like if they lied all the time, then removing them was my best course of action.

The first time I ever fired someone, I was a nervous wreck and I felt like a jerk.

This feeling did not make sense since this employee had consistently demonstrated a lack of integrity and did not appear to care about her job. She consistently showed up late and then accomplished little while she was there.

I later realized my negative feelings were coming from my historic baggage. Once I changed how I viewed her removal, I felt better. She was miserable working there. Letting her go could be the most helpful thing I could do for her. I was giving her an opportunity to find employment someplace where she might be happier. Whether she found better employment was outside my control, but at least I was giving her the motivation she needed to go and look for it.

When I have supported and protected my staff and treated them with honesty, integrity, compassion, empathy, and competence, they were able to collaborate and cooperate with each other and became a synergistic team that supported the company's productivity.

Others

As an employee and representative of a company, I always felt it was important to demonstrate my trustworthiness in all my interactions with people associated with the company, including customers, vendors, bankers, and anyone else doing business with us.

One of my goals was to strengthen the relationships the company had with people outside the organization.

For example, when I was doing collection work for the mortgage servicing company, I tried to establish a bond between the company and each delinquent mortgagee. My job was not to badger the mortgagee into sending us money. My job was to try and help them solve the problem of bringing their payments current and keeping them current. I wanted them to feel good about my phone call, not harassed by it. This was the viewpoint I convinced the other collectors to use which improved all our productivity and morale.

To build healthy relationships with the people outside of the companies where I worked, I consistently tried to interact with them with honesty, integrity, compassion, empathy, and competence.

Growing a Successful Business

I came to view a business as simply a collection of relationships, and I found the secret to growing a successful business was building healthy relationships with everyone involved with it.

For example, imagine the owner of a successful business sitting at her desk in her corner office overlooking the city. Narrow beams of light radiate out from her and connect her to each person with whom she has a business relationship.

There is a separate beam of light connecting her to each one of her customers. There is a separate beam of light connecting her to each one of her vendors. There is a separate beam of light connecting her to each one of her employees. And there is a separate beam of light connecting her to each one of her investors, lenders, and everyone else associated with her business.

She has thousands of beams of light, some traveling around the world. Some of the beams extend from her to an employee and then from that employee to a customer, or a lender, or someone else connected to her business. Although one beam of light may pass through many different people, it still originates with her and represents a business relationship of hers.

Now imagine her before she started her business. She has no office, no business relationships, and no beams of light. Perhaps she is alone and struggling with a problem in her life. Although she has shopped for a solution, she has been unable to find one. So, using her imagination, she figures out how to solve the problem herself.

For years, she shares her solution with people she meets who are struggling with the same problem.

One day, she reads a quote by Peter Diamandis:

> *Want to become a billionaire?*
> *Then help a billion people.*

She thinks about her solution to that problem and realizes it might make a good business. Although she has no desire to become a billionaire, she likes helping people, and she thinks if she starts a business and helps enough people, the business might become successful.

The birth of every business takes place inside the imagination of one individual. And at this moment, she has built her first business relationship. It is with herself.

As she thinks about starting a business, though, she realizes she does not trust herself to do it because she does not know how.

When she discusses her idea with her family and friends, some of them encourage her to start the business and a few provide her with technical and financial assistance. Without planning to, she has converted some of her personal relationships into business relationships. This is when she realizes she does not need to know everything about starting a business because she trusts herself to find trustworthy people who will help her do it.

Next, she builds a business relationship with a consultant who helps her create a business plan. Then she builds relationships with potential investors. A new relationship with a landlord provides her with an office to rent. Then she builds a relationship with an employment agency who provides her with her first employee. She builds a healthy relationship with her employee who then builds relationships with vendors who provide office furnishings and advertising.

Eventually, our business owner meets and builds a healthy relationship with her first customer. Then she meets and builds a healthy relationship with another customer, and another, and another.

Over the years, the volume of her relationships grows. Her business helps thousands of people, and it becomes a bigger success than she had ever imagined.

Now, she sits in her corner office overlooking the city and has thousands of business relationships around the world.

Healthy Relationships = Business Growth

I believe the secret for growing any successful business is growing healthy relationships. And to grow healthy relationships, each one must be built on mutual trust and be mutually beneficial regardless if it is with a customer, a vendor, an employee, an investor, or someone outside the business.

The size of a successful business can be measured by the quantity of their healthy relationships. Healthy relationships tend to last a long time because they are mutually beneficial. When both parties benefit from a relationship, they both want it to continue.

If a business owner does not build healthy, long-term, mutually beneficial relationships, then their business will struggle to replace the relationships they lose. They will be unable to increase the overall quantity of their relationships, and their business will not grow.

If they do build healthy, long-term, mutually beneficial relationships, those relationships will stay with them. And every new relationship they build will then add to their existing relationships, thereby increasing the overall size and success of their business.

Building a successful business really is this simple.

Of course, there are a lot of other things that have to be done like execution, research, development, process improvement, accounting, human resources, legal, taxes, and things of that nature, but a business owner can always hire trustworthy people who can take care of all that for them.

Summary

Co-workers include everyone with whom I have worked. They include peers, bosses, employees who have reported to me, and people outside the companies including customers and vendors. A healthy co-worker relationship is one that is mutually beneficial and built on mutual trust.

When I have viewed my peers and boss as members of my team and treated them with honesty, integrity, compassion, empathy, and competence, then I was able to build healthy, productive, and long-term mutually beneficial relationships with them.

If my boss did not respond well to my trustworthiness, then I needed to find employment elsewhere.

When I was the boss, supporting and protecting my staff were my top priorities.

Treating outside people associated with the company where I worked with honesty, integrity, compassion, empathy, and competence built healthy relationships which were important to the overall success of the company.

* * *

Before reading the next chapter, you might want to try these Co-workers Exercises:

Co-Workers Exercises

Improve the health of your relationship with a peer.

1. Make a list of some things you could do you think your peer would appreciate.

2. Pick one item on the list and do it.
3. Make a note of what happened.
4. Pick another item on the list and do it soon.
5. Make a note of what happened.
6. Review the list and make any adjustments based on your new experience with your peer.
7. Repeat steps 2-7 until your relationship with your peer improves, or you are convinced it never will.

Improve the health of your relationship with your boss.
1. Make a list of things you could do you think your boss would appreciate.
2. Pick one item on the list and do it.
3. Make a note of what happened.
4. Pick another item on the list and do it soon.
5. Make a note of what happened.
6. Review the list and make any adjustments based on your new experience with your boss.
7. Repeat steps 2-7 until your relationship with your boss improves, or you are convinced it never will.

Improve the health of your relationships with your employees by supporting them.
1. Ask your employees what they think you could get for them that would improve their performance.
2. Pick one item on their list and get it for them as soon as possible.
3. Make a note of their response.

4. Pick another item and get it for them as soon as possible.
5. Make a note of their response.
6. Review their list and make any adjustments based on your new experience with your employees.
7. Repeat steps 2-7 until your relationships with your employees improve.

Improve the health of your relationships with your employees by protecting them.
1. Evaluate the trustworthiness of each employee and decide which one is the least trustworthy.
2. Specifically list why.
3. List what you can do to improve that employee's trustworthiness.
4. Pick one item on the list and do it.
5. Did it improve their trustworthiness?
6. Repeat steps 4-6 until their trustworthiness improves or you are convinced it never will.
7. If you cannot improve their trustworthiness to an acceptable level, politely terminate their employment with empathy.
8. How did the rest of the staff respond?
9. Repeat steps 1-9 until you only have trustworthy employees.

Study Group Questions

1. Would anyone like to share your experience working alongside a bad employee? What made them a bad employee?
2. Would anyone like to share your experience working for a bad boss? What made them a bad boss?
3. Would anyone like to share your experience firing a bad employee? How did it make you feel?
4. Would anyone like to share your experience dealing with a difficult customer? How did your boss respond?
5. Would anyone like to share your experience trying to grow a business?
6. Would anyone like to share your experience with the Co-Workers Exercises?

Chapter 16

Acquaintances

I consider everyone I know, who is not a loved-one or a co-worker, to be an acquaintance. This group spans a wide range of relationships.

At one end of the range are people I call my friends, but whom I do not love, like most of my friends on Facebook. I like them, but I do not love them, and we rarely visit.

In the middle of the range are people I barely know, like many of my neighbors. We wave and exchange greetings, but I only know some of their names. Since I know little else about them, I would not call them my friends.

At the far end of the range are people I know but do not trust, like an old friend of mine. When he started to allow his addictions to influence his decision making, I decided I could no longer trust him to be in my life.

I believe a healthy relationship with an acquaintance is one where I trust them only as much as they are worthy of my trust, and we each invest time and energy into our relationship that is proportional to the benefit we each derive from it.

For example, my Facebook friends do not take up much of my time, and I enjoy many of their posts and photos. Most of my neighbors are friendly, and I enjoy exchanging pleasantries with them. It makes me feel good to think I live in a friendly neighborhood. The people I know, but do not trust, I just try to avoid for I see no mutual benefit from spending any time with them.

In the past, I had some acquaintances who demanded more of my time than I felt was appropriate. They would refer to me as their friend and constantly try to pull me away from whatever I might be doing so I would help them with their problems. I eventually decided I should not allow that to happen anymore.

For example, I had a neighbor who never solved his own problems and constantly asked for my assistance while never offering his assistance to me. Understanding mutual trust helped me to reconsider my relationship with him. I needed to somehow balance the time-invested versus the benefits-received scale in our relationship.

The next few times he asked me to help him, I said something like, "I'm sorry, but I'm busy with a family project. Let me get back to you when I'm done." Then, I would wait at least two days before getting back to him. By then, most of the time he had already gotten someone else to do what he wanted me to do.

During this same time, I called him whenever I was doing something with which I thought he might be able to help me. He frequently came over and helped, and his increased contribution to our relationship balanced the scale and made our relationship healthier.

I started requiring all my relationships with my acquaintances to be mutually beneficial, otherwise I knew they would not be healthy or long-term.

Summary

Acquaintances are all the people I know who are not loved-ones or co-workers. They include some friends, people I barely know, and people I know but do not trust.

A healthy relationship with an acquaintance is one where I trust them only as much as they are worthy of my trust, and we both invest time and energy into our relationship that is proportional to the benefit we each derive from it.

*   *   *

Before reading the next chapter, you might want to try these Acquaintances Exercises:

Acquaintances Exercises

Improve the health of your relationship with an acquaintance.

1. Make two lists. One, things you can do you think your acquaintance will appreciate. Two, things your acquaintance can do you will appreciate.
2. Pick one item on the first list and do it tomorrow.
3. Make a note of what happened.
4. Pick one item on the second list and ask your acquaintance to help you with it the next day.
5. Make a note of what happened.
6. Review the lists and make any adjustments based on your new experience with your acquaintance.
7. Wait a week or so and pick another item on the first list and do it.
8. Make a note of what happened.

9. Wait another week and pick one item on the second list and ask your acquaintance to help you with it.
10. Make a note of what happened.
11. Repeat steps 6-11 until your relationship with your acquaintance improves, or you are convinced it never will.

Improve your relationship with an acquaintance who wants more of your time than you feel is appropriate.
1. Say *no* to their requests more often than you do now.
2. Ask them for their help more often than you do now.
3. Repeat steps 1 and 2 until you feel better about your relationship with them, or you are convinced you never will.

Study Group Questions

1. How do you feel about the relationship group of *Acquaintances* being so broad?
2. Would anyone like to share your experience with a needy acquaintance? How did you handle it?
3. Would anyone like to share your experience with the Acquaintances Exercises?

Chapter 17

Strangers

A stranger is anyone I do not know, and the world is full of them.

I severely limit the trust I grant to strangers because I do not know if they are trustworthy. If I meet a stranger and get to know them a little, I might determine it is safe to trust them a little, but that would only be because they would no longer be a stranger. They would, at the very least, have become an acquaintance.

I know I will never have relationships with most of the strangers with whom I share this planet. There is simply not enough time in my lifetime. However, since I do not live in a town where I know everyone, I do interact with strangers on most days.

Whether a stranger is tallying my purchases at a grocery store, standing in line with me to get coffee, taking my order at a restaurant, sitting by me in a theater, or driving down the same road as I am, maintaining a healthy relationship with them is important if I hope to have a good day.

I have read many stories of people's days having been ruined by getting into conflicts with strangers, and I do not wish to become one of them.

Since a stranger is someone I do not know, I do not trust them beyond the scope of our current interaction.

For example, if I have never met my waitress, trusting her to take my dinner order is reasonable. However, trusting her to borrow my car is not. That does not mean I actively distrust her. Just because I do not know her does not mean I need to worry about her poisoning my food.

A healthy relationship with a stranger is more about not offending them than it is about trusting them. The social skills I discussed in chapter ten work wonders when I interact with strangers.

In general, I try to do the following with strangers:

- Be friendly, but not trust them as I would my friends
- Be kind, but not overly generous
- Be courteous, but not so much as to appear haughty
- Be nice, but maintain a high level of skepticism

Protecting Myself from Scams

Thanks to advancements in communication technology, I can use texts, low-cost long-distance calling, internet video conferencing, and social media postings to stay in contact with people all over the globe. Maintaining long-distance relationships has never been easier.

Unfortunately, these same advancements have empowered international criminals to communicate directly to me every day in hopes of catching me at a vulnerable moment so they can take advantage of me.

Criminals are looking for any vulnerable person who might have their guard down, if even for a moment. And a moment is all a professional con artist needs to gain someone's trust because they are trained to appear trustworthy.

For example, they target families who have lost loved-ones with stories of unpaid bills. They target senior citizens with stories of their grandchildren needing help. They target people with things listed for sale with stories of wanting to buy whatever they have listed.

Criminals will say anything to get people to trust them.

I used to think scams only happened to other people, but when a criminal happened to catch me at just the right moment, I was vulnerable to their lies too. Twenty-five years ago, I bought a $1,200 vacuum cleaner from a door-to-door salesman because he convinced me my son needed a cleaner house to keep his allergies and ADHD under control. The salesman pushed the right buttons at just the right time and succeeded in separating me from my money.

Trusting strangers is more dangerous now than it has ever been because I am exposed to more criminals now than ever before. I now view any communication from a stranger with a critical eye, regardless if it arrives as a letter in my mailbox, a text on my phone, an email, a voicemail, a social media post, or a knock on my door. Every week, I receive numerous messages from people telling me I have been approved for a loan, or the IRS is starting legal action against me, or money has been found that belongs to me, or whatever the latest scam happens to be. Every week.

And that does not include all the phone calls I ignore. Sometimes, my caller ID displays a number that looks similar to mine. The scammers are hoping I will answer their call if the number looks local or familiar. They have the technology to make the caller ID show any number they want. One time, I received a call and the caller ID listed my own phone number, like I was calling myself.

I find it creepy to think so many people sit around trying to dream up ways of stealing from others. They could probably use that same energy to dream up ways of helping others and make a great living at it. But no, they prefer to scam people.

Even though the number of creeps out there trying to reach me has increased, I do not think the percentage of strangers who are creeps has increased. That percentage is probably about the same. It is just that technology has made it easier for the creeps to reach out to more people. So, I am probably just hearing from a larger percentage of the already existing creeps.

I am hopeful someone will eventually figure out a way to put a stop to the billions of emails, phone calls, and text messages that criminals generate. In the meantime, all I can do is try to stay aware and do my best to protect myself.

Here is what I do to avoid being scammed:

- Never trust a stranger, unless they prove to me I can trust them (through their actions, not just their words).
- Never click on a link sent by a stranger.

- Never click on a link sent by someone I know unless I am expecting it, or I call them first and verify they sent it.
- Never open an email attachment sent by a stranger.
- Never open an email attachment sent by someone I know unless I am expecting it, or I call them first and verify they sent it.
- Never answer my phone if I do not recognize the number of the caller. If it is important, they can leave a message and I will call them back.
- Never call a phone number left by a stranger. Instead, I look up the official number and call it. A close friend of mine received a voicemail from someone claiming to be from the police department. When she called the number they had left, someone answered it as if it was the police department. It was not.
- If I answer my phone and a pre-recorded message starts playing, I hang up immediately. I do not care what the message says. If it is prerecorded, I doubt if it is for me anyway.
- Never give a stranger personal information, including my social security number, log-in information, passwords, or financial information.

- Never send money to a stranger, including cash, check, wire, gift card, credit card, or bank transfer, regardless of the reason they say I should.

Summary

A stranger is anyone I do not know. I severely limit the trust I give them until I know they are worthy of my trust. A healthy relationship with a stranger is more about not offending them than it is about trusting them.

Advancements in technology have increased the reach of international criminals requiring an increased skepticism on my part toward strangers.

* * *

Before reading the next chapter, you might want to try this Strangers Exercise:

Strangers Exercise

1. For the next 24 hours, be more friendly and polite to the strangers you meet than you normally would.
2. Note how they respond and how that makes you feel.
3. Think about a good interaction you have had with a stranger. What did you do that contributed to the interaction being good?
4. Think about a bad interaction you have had with a stranger. What did you do that contributed to the interaction being bad?

5. Looking back on that experience, how would you act differently now?

Study Group Questions

1. What can we do to improve our interactions with strangers?
2. What vulnerabilities do we have that might make us susceptible to being scammed?
3. What can we do to protect ourselves from being scammed?
4. Would anyone like to share your experience with the Strangers Exercise?

Chapter 18

Soulmates

After finishing that last chapter, I realize I do not want to end this book on a negative discussion about trying to avoid scams. So, on a more positive note, I am going to discuss the subject of soulmates.

I define a soulmate as someone I deeply trust, someone with whom I can deeply relate, and someone with whom I want to share the rest of my life. Corky is my soulmate. We have been living together since 1974. We trust each other completely and benefit greatly from each other's support and love. I feel fortunate to have found her so early in my life.

I believe anyone can find at least one soulmate because I believe there are many potential soulmates out there for each person. And a soulmate is not necessarily someone with whom you have sex. You can have a life-long platonic relationship with a soulmate, like a best friend you love dearly.

If there are multiple, potential soulmates out there for everyone, then you might wonder, "What can I do to find one of mine and build a healthy relationship with them?"

Here are my three simple steps to do exactly that:

1. Become more trustworthy
2. Look for someone who is worthy of your trust and trusts you in return
3. Love them

Chapters two through ten explain how you can become more trustworthy. If you learn and practice that material, you will have the first step covered.

Chapter eleven explains what to look for when evaluating the trustworthiness of someone. If you learn and practice that material, you will have most of the second step covered. Please note, however, the first two words of step two are *look for*. No one can find a soulmate if they do not *look for* one. That means using your self-awareness, long-term perspective, and self-control to open yourself up to the possibility you can find someone with whom you can share your life and that it is worth your time and energy to look.

Of course, your DNA-soup and historic baggage may provide all manner of reasons and emotions to stop you, but you do not have to listen to them. You might feel scared or nervous since you cannot control your emotions, but your emotions do not control you. You decide your actions, and it is your actions that determine your future, not your emotions.

Although the first step to finding a soulmate is to take whatever time you need to learn and practice becoming more trustworthy, you should not use your lack of perfection as an excuse. You will never be perfect. Perfection is an unrealistic expectation. You should only be trying to improve.

Once you are more trustworthy and are confident you can spot trustworthiness in others, then you are ready to look for a soulmate. But where do you look?

To find a soulmate, you will need to convert one of your existing relationships into something more than it is right now. So, you might as well start with those people you already love, like your closest friends.

Corky and I were close friends for five months before we became a couple. And we were a couple for ten months before we got married and committed ourselves to being life partners and soulmates.

The most important thing for you to look for in a soulmate is a person who is worthy of your trust. Nothing else matters. The person's height does not matter. The person's age does not matter. The person's gender does not matter. The color of the person's skin does not matter. How physically attractive the person is does not matter. When you are looking for a soulmate, you are looking for someone with whom you can share your life. All that matters is:

- Does that person act with honesty?
- Does that person act with integrity?
- Does that person act with compassion?
- Does that person act with empathy?
- Does that person act with competence?

If there are no candidates among your closest friends, how about co-workers? Corky and I worked together before we became close friends.

If not co-workers, then how about acquaintances? By reaching out and communicating with them empathetically, many acquaintances will respond, providing you with an opportunity to get to know them better. By spending time with an acquaintance, that acquaintance could become a close friend. With continued interaction and the building of mutual trust, that close friend could become a soulmate, even if the relationship stays platonic.

If your relationship groups of loved-ones, co-workers, and acquaintances, contain no potential soulmates, then all that is left for you are about seven billion strangers. I would think the odds are pretty good at least of few of them would be potential soulmates for you.

Personally, I have always found the idea of meeting a stranger to be terrifying. In 1974, my solution was to join a group of strangers with whom I shared a common passion. A shared passion is a great way to bond with strangers and convert them into acquaintances, co-workers, and loved-ones. Even though Scientology's so-called *technology* did not appear to be all L. Ron Hubbard claimed it was, the people involved were passionate and dedicated to helping people. By joining them, I met a soulmate. Prior to joining Scientology, I had not had a girlfriend (or even a close friend) in two years.

If you are going to look at strangers as potential soulmates, I would advise you to keep your skepticism on its highest alert level. You should be on the lookout for anything that would indicate a lack of trustworthiness because if you are not careful, you could end up in a cult.

Wait, that is what happened to me. Oops. In my defense, that was before I had compiled all the material for this book. And yet, joining that cult still helped me find a soulmate.

If I were looking for a soulmate today, I would research each group before joining. And I would continue to research groups until I found one I wanted to join.

I have read many stories about people who have found soulmates on internet dating sites. I even know one couple who met through one and have been happily married for over twelve years. However, I know far more people who have wasted hundreds of hours with no luck whatsoever. One of the biggest problems with searching for a soulmate on an internet dating site is it can be difficult to spot dishonesty. A friend of mine had spent many hours trying to establish a relationship with a person who, as it turned out, had posted someone else's photo as their own.

If you do decide to try an internet dating site, please keep your skepticism alert level on maximum. Scam artists patrol them, and you do not want to be their next victim.

I would think using the internet to find a group worthy of joining would be the safer bet, especially since joining a group is what worked for me.

Another idea that might work (even if it does sound a bit self-serving since I am the author), you could start a study group and invite potential soulmates to join you in the study of this book. The study group meetings would provide ample opportunity to interact with your candidate(s) while discussing trust. Of course, when the group discusses this paragraph, your potential soulmate(s) may become suspicious, but that could provide you with an opportunity to be honest about why you started the group.

Who knows what might happen?

Once you do find a potential soulmate, you should take your time and get to know them. You want to verify your candidate really is worthy of your trust, and as your candidate gets to know you, they can recognize your trustworthiness also. As you become more confident the trust is mutual and the relationship is beneficial to you both, you slowly increase the third step.

You love them.

As discussed in chapter fourteen, I am not talking about falling in love with them as in feeling the emotion of love. I am talking about love as a verb. It is something you do. You love them, whether your relationship is sexual or not. That means you treat them with more and more honesty, integrity, compassion, empathy, and competence until you are loving them:

All the time.

And when that happens, both your lives improve.

Summary

I believe many soulmates exist for each person. If you do not have a soulmate, you just need to find one of yours. My three simple steps to finding and building a healthy relationship with a potential soulmate are:

1. Become more trustworthy
2. Look for someone who is worthy of your trust and trusts you in return
3. Love them

* * *

Before setting this book aside, you might want to try these Soulmates Exercises:

Soulmates Exercises

If you already have a soulmate.
1. Write down how you feel about them.
2. Write down why your soulmate deserves your love.
3. Write down a list of things you can do you think your soulmate would appreciate.
4. Pick one item on the list and do it tomorrow.
5. Write down what happened when you did it. How did you feel? How did they respond? Was it a good choice?
6. Update your list based on your new understanding.
7. Pick another item and do it the next day.
8. Write down what happened when you did it. How did you feel? How did they respond? Was it a good choice?
9. Update your list based on your new understanding.
10. Repeat steps 4-10 for the rest of your life.

If you do not yet have a soulmate.
1. Think about your closest friends. Could any one of them be a potential soulmate?
2. If not, skip to step 14.
3. If so, engage your self-awareness and ask yourself this question, "Why does this potential soulmate deserve my love?"

4. Write down how you feel and what you think about this question.
5. Write down your answer to the question.
6. Write down a list of things you can do you think this person would appreciate.
7. Pick one item on the list and do it tomorrow.
8. Write down what happened when you did it. How did you feel? How did they respond? Was it a good choice?
9. Update your list based on your new understanding.
10. Pick another item and do it the next day.
11. Write down what happened when you did it. How did you feel? How did they respond? Was it a good choice?
12. Update your list based on your new understanding.
13. Repeat steps 7-13 until this person becomes your soulmate or they convince you they never will.
14. If you do not think any of your closest friends could be a potential soulmate, then think about your co-workers. Could any one of them be a potential soulmate?
15. If not, skip to step 17.
16. If so, apply the appropriate Co-Workers Exercise to them from chapter fifteen.
17. If you do not think any of your co-workers could be a potential soulmate, then think about your acquaintances. Could any one of them be a potential soulmate?

18. If not, skip to step 20.
19. If so, apply the first Acquaintances Exercise to them from chapter sixteen.
20. If you do not think any of your acquaintances could be a potential soulmate, then find a group of passionate people who interest you.
21. Attend one of their meetings.
22. If you cannot relate to the group, then skip to step 25.
23. If you can relate to the group, then participate and see if anyone is a potential soulmate.
24. Apply the first Acquaintances Exercise to them from chapter sixteen.
25. If you cannot relate to the group or you do not see any of the members as a potential soulmate, then find another group of passionate people who interest you.
26. Repeat steps 21-26 until you find a soulmate.

Study Group Questions

1. Would anyone like to share a successful experience finding a soulmate?
2. Would anyone like to share your frustration trying to find a soulmate?
3. Does anyone have a group of passionate people that interests you?
4. Would anyone like to share your experience with the Soulmates Exercises?

Contact Information

I hope you found this information helpful. If you have any questions or comments, please email me at:

Tim@ShortridgeBusinessServices.com

A Special Request from the Author

I have spent the last couple of years compiling and organizing this material and then writing and rewriting this book because I strongly believe this information can help people improve the relationships in their lives.

If you have found this book helpful, would you please do me a favor and write an online review of it? Your review could help other people find this book and receive the same benefits from it you have. The more reviews a book receives, the easier it is for readers to find it.

Thank you. I appreciate it.

Acknowledgements

This book would not have been possible without the support and assistance of my wife, best friend, and soulmate, Corky Shortridge. She also happens to be my editor, proof-reader, and best critic.

Our daughter, Melanie, also provided valuable feedback to early drafts of both the first and final chapters.

Thank you both. Thank you, thank you, thank you.

Other Books by
Tim Shortridge

Non-fiction

DON'T COOK FISH in the Company Microwave
 – Career Advice

Do you look forward to going to work? If not, this book could help.

With a dash of humor, this book describes five simple steps to doing well and feeling good at work. It also includes 335 secrets and tips to help you advance your career (and which might just improve your life).

I have stumbled in my career so many times it is embarrassing. Each time, it cost me dearly, either in time, money, or both. Mostly both. I wrote this book for my children because I did not want them to duplicate the career mistakes I had made. I have now made it available hoping it helps you too. – Tim Shortridge

UNDERSTAND ACCOUNTING
Without Falling Asleep

– Accounting Primer

Learn the basics in just 47 pages. When humor meets accounting, understanding wins. So, have a little fun while you learn.

In 1992, I started my own business setting up accounting systems for small businesses and teaching the owners how to use them. Over the years, I developed this simple explanation of accounting basics that has proven effective with my non-accountant clients. Not only do they understand basic accounting, but they also stay awake during the learning process. – Tim Shortridge

UNDERSTAND California
Sales & Use Tax

– Sales Tax Basics & Tracking

Understanding and tracking sales and use taxes is a thorn in the side of most businesses. This book brings simplicity and clarity to a complex subject.

NO PLACE TO RUN
– Holocaust Memoir

David and Sophie Goetzel moved
from Germany to Warsaw, Poland
in 1937 to escape the rising Nazi
anti-Semitism at home. When the
Germans invaded two years later,
David vowed to keep his loved-
ones alive.

With dogged determination, the help of people he
befriended along the way, and luck, he guided his wife
and two-year-old daughter through the siege of Warsaw,
imprisonment by the Gestapo, confinement in the
Warsaw ghetto, going into hiding on the Aryan side of
the city, eventual internment in Bergen-Belsen, and a
terrifying train ride that led to liberation in 1945.

David, his wife, and his daughter all survived.

*Michael D. Frounfelter and I wrote this true story about
my friend, David Gilbert, in the style of a suspense /
thriller. We have been told it reads as if John Grisham
had written* **The Diary of Anne Frank***, but with a happy
ending. – Tim Shortridge*

Fiction

SEALING FATE – Suspense Novel

There is an arsonist on the loose in San Diego County igniting wildfires in the dry, overgrown canyons whenever the Santa Ana winds blow. Doctor Vanessa Tornen lives with her mother and daughter in a house that overlooks one of those canyons.

When Doctor Tornen completes her OB/GYN residency and accepts a position at a women's center, she thinks she may have found a job that will allow her to begin paying down her massive student loan debt and finally start getting her personal life together. Then a group of pro-life fanatics decides to shut down the women's center by harassing the employees and their families.

Doctor Tornen's entire world could come crashing down around her, if it does not go up in flames first.

JAKE – Children's Bedtime Story

Small dog. Big personality.
With 22 full-color pages of
humorous pictures and doggie
monologue, JAKE is a great
bedtime story book. It also
makes a perfect gift for any
beginning reader.

OUT OF PLUMB – Humorous
Poems and Short Stories

Need a quick laugh? This
humorous collection of
quirkiness will have you
chuckling in no time.